Sub-Saharan African Immigrants' Stories of Resilience and Courage

Mariam Konaté and Fredah Mainah

ANTHEM PRESS

Anthem Press
An imprint of Wimbledon Publishing Company
www.anthempress.com

This edition first published in UK and USA 2023
by ANTHEM PRESS
75–76 Blackfriars Road, London SE1 8HA, UK
or PO Box 9779, London SW19 7ZG, UK
and
244 Madison Ave #116, New York, NY 10016, USA

British Library Cataloguing-in-Publication Data
A catalogue record for this book is available from the British Library.

Library of Congress Cataloging-in-Publication Data
A catalog record for this book has been requested.

ISBN-13: 978-1-83998-786-1 (Hbk)
ISBN-10: 1-83998-786-3 (Hbk)

Cover Credit: franz12/Shutterstock.com.

This title is also available as an e-book.

CONTENTS

LIST OF FIGURES AND TABLES

ACKNOWLEDGEMENTS

The final shape of the book owes much to the care and guidance of our editors at Anthem Press. We are also grateful to Vanessa Davies of https://www.vrhdavies.com/ for her meticulous editing and proofing skills that greatly benefitted us.

We thank Manuel Soque, PhD, for all the help he provided to proofread and edit the raw manuscript while it was in the writing phase. Most of all, we are forever grateful to our sub-Saharan African immigrants who were interviewed for this book.

DEDICATION

To our children, the second generation of sub-Saharan immigrants: Sonnie, Reuben, Aisha, Muhammad, and Fatimata. We dedicate this book to you and hope that you will realize your American dream beyond our wildest imaginations.

To all immigrants, for all your resilience and courage.

FOREWORD

This book outlines challenges faced by sub-Saharan African immigrants here presented in their voices. The researchers interviewed and had deep conversations with 25 immigrants from sub-Saharan Africa and present those conversations and their findings in the following chapters.

In Chapter 1, the authors introduce the problem statement of their research against the backdrop of African immigration trends and punitive United States immigration policies in a historical background of trade in enslaved Africans and current policies on the continent. The purpose of the study, its significance, scope, and the literature that was reviewed are also discussed.

The authors use Chapter 2 to discuss and reflect on the challenges of using phenomenology as a research design and maintaining unbiased interconnection as both researchers and objects of research, and still being able to give a voice to nameless and countless stories of sub-Saharan African immigrants in the United States. This phenomenological research chapter provides trends of immigration and valuable insights into the multifaceted stories of sub-Saharan Africans in the United States and their varied and personal stories of perseverance, courage, and survival strategies. This chapter details the procedure used to conduct research for this book and the challenges the researchers encountered while taking on the double role of researcher and participant.

Among the many challenges the sub-Saharan African immigrants face is the issue of being viewed as different yet expected to assimilate and behave as an American. To delve deeper into the identity crises that many African immigrants are experiencing, the authors use Chapter 3 to discuss the issue of translanguaging and code switching, which is a common communication and coping style among most plurilinguals. It also deals with the difficult reality of the lack of validation that many immigrants feel in the United States. Indeed, the authors' research shows that many of the respondents feel like their lived experiences are being discounted, just because they are different.

In Chapter 4, the authors introduce identity issues by exploring how sub-Saharan African immigrants perceive and define success. The major reason cited for immigrating was education, which was also perceived as a definition of as well as a criterion of success.

Chapter 5 delves deeper into the challenges of coming to the United States and being confronted by issues of race, national narratives adopted to describe all peoples of color, and discrimination along color lines.

In Chapter 6, the authors expound identity issues by discussing some disturbing trends of behavior that seem to be used to deal with critical identity issues. Here the authors explore a variety of issues, including the use of hair extensions, straightening of hair, fitting in, assimilation and integration, and the phenomenon of skin bleaching that is used globally to whiten and depigment themselves as a strategy of coping and fitting in. The authors discuss the issues related to the inner struggles that sub-Saharan African immigrants experience in trying to navigate between two worlds and values. This chapter also explores the issues of trying to assimilate and fit in the American culture, negotiating race, class, and gender biases and other plurilingual challenges.

In Chapter 7, the authors discuss the dilemma faced by sub-Saharan African immigrants, the paradox and myth of going back to their native country after graduation or "making it." While other researchers on African immigration suggest that major reasons for immigration are economic, war, or conflict related, most of the respondents interviewed gave education and family reunification as their main reasons for emigrating. Furthermore, the myth of going back home shows that the pursuit of education was to position them for better job opportunities back in their native countries. The researchers reflect on the myth held by many immigrants in the United States: the hope of one day going back home after completing education or getting the needed resources.

The main argument that the researchers are making in Chapter 8 is that current leadership styles and disillusionment with leaders in some of the sub-Saharan African countries was a major immigration factor for some of the respondents.

Chapter 9 is an opportunity for the authors to reflect on the major themes from the research especially that of leadership and their personal leadership experiences. This chapter further makes a few suggestions on how to improve leadership by focusing on leader development in African countries. This chapter brings to the fore leadership challenges that the researchers have encountered as well as their futuristic approach to handling those issues.

The last section of the book concludes and presents the researchers' plans for coaching and mentoring using their own devised model and technique. Here the researchers outline a coaching model and pedagogy they intend to use to coach and mentor future leaders. Suggestions for further research are also made in this concluding section.

Chapter 1

INTRODUCTION AND BACKGROUND

*To this day we continue to lose the best among ourselves because the lights
in the developed world shine brighter.*

—Nelson Mandela

*I've always felt that it is impossible to engage properly with a place or a person without
engaging with all of the stories of that place and that person. The consequence of
the single story is this: it robs people of dignity. It makes our recognition of our equal
humanity difficult. It emphasizes how we are different rather than how we are similar.*
—Chimamanda Adichie, 2009 TED Global

If we were to assess Africa's development the way we assess that of a person,
starting at the point where Africa's existence first appears in written records,
rather than the geological history of the planet—from birth, naming and through
all the stages to the present—Africa's identity would be much more understood
and appreciated. Through the many courses of human history, the land
and peoples of Africa have faced—and continue to face—many challenges.
Fortunately, Africa is a huge and very resilient continent that continues to grow
and change regardless of the centuries of plunder, genocides, and demeaning
policies thrown at the land and people and all the beings that reside and depend
on it.

In the last three or so decades, there has been an increased historical
interest in Africa. As the oldest inhabited continent on Earth, Africa is home
to all humankind. Archaeological evidence indicates that humans and
human ancestors have lived in Africa for more than 5 million years.
African diversity in genetic makeup is also uncontested. Britannica records
that some of the oldest traces of life have been identified in the Transvaal
region of South Africa, preserved as unicellular algae in rocks dating
from 3.4 to 2.6 billion years ago, placing the life forms firmly during
the Precambrian era, which extended from 4.6 billion to 541 million years
ago (Windley 2020; Nicol et al. 2021).

Anthropological and archaeological records indicate that Africa is the oldest inhabited continent, the site where fossil evidence of human beings (*Homo sapiens*) and their ancestors, with evidence of critical evolution stages, has been found. Africa is one of the most linguistically diverse continents in the world. It has more than 2,000 languages and is home to more countries than any other continent (Brown and Ogilvie 2010). More than 50 percent of the world's French-speaking population lives on the African continent, and Angola has more Portuguese speakers than Portugal, not to mention that English speakers outside Britain are more than its population (UN Security Council 2020). According to the United Nations and the International Monetary Fund (IMF), sub-Saharan Africa is the area south of the Sahara Desert, excluding Egypt, Libya, Algeria, Morocco, Tunisia, and Sudan, however absurd and racist this categorization is. The African continent has 54 countries, including Morocco, Western Sahara, Algeria, Tunisia, Libya, Egypt, Sudan, South Sudan, Chad, Niger, Mali, Mauritania, Senegal, The Gambia, Guinea-Bissau, Guinea, Sierra Leone, Liberia, Côte d'Ivoire, Ghana, Burkina Faso, Togo, Benin, Nigeria, Cameroon, Central Africa Republic, Equatorial Guinea, Gabon, Congo, Democratic Republic of the Congo, Angola, Namibia, Botswana, South Africa, Lesotho, Eswatini, Mozambique, Zimbabwe, Zambia, Malawi, Tanzania, Rwanda, Burundi, Uganda, Kenya, Somalia, Ethiopia, Djibouti, Eritrea, and the island countries of Cape Verde, Sao Tome e Principe, Madagascar, Mauritius, Seychelles, and Comoros.

Out of these, we interviewed 25 participants from the major migration countries and regions of sub-Saharan African immigrants: *West Africa* (Nigeria [3], Burkina Faso [2], and Senegal [1]), *Eastern Africa* (Kenya [11], Uganda [3], Rwanda [1], and Ethiopia [2]), and *Southern Africa* (Botswana [1] and Zambia [1]).

Africa is the second largest continent, after Asia. It has a landmass of 1.73 million square miles and a population of 1.4 billion people, with billions of other beings across 54 countries (Khapoya 2013). However, despite its large size, population, and well-documented rich flora and fauna, Africa often finds itself defined by others in negative terms, unless of course from an economic perspective, when Africa's grain- and mineral-rich resources are seen as a boon. The commonly used Mercator projection distorts the relative sizes of land masses so that Africa appears much smaller than it is in reality. Others, such as the Gall–Peters projection, use a different formulation to present landmasses, with quite different results from the Mercator (for the original publication, see Gall 1885). The continent of Africa is surrounded by the Mediterranean Sea, the Red Sea, the Indian Ocean, and the Atlantic Ocean; has many large freshwater lakes and rivers for water sources; is bisected by the Equator;

and is home to the Sahara Desert, tropical forests, savannahs, and towering mountain ranges, many topped by glaciers, giving the continent an abundance of biodiversity (UNEP-WCMC 2016).

Those of us who are proud to be associated with this great continent frame our identity around it and call ourselves Africans, despite the shady history of the origin of that name. Our identities are also complicated by the naming and artificial boundaries created by European colonizers. However, we have come to understand what Shakespeare meant about a rose by any other name. After all, the legacy of colonialism continues, and the naming systems of the peoples of the African continent have been corrupted. We take on Eurocentric names to fit in like that poor kid who was bullied in school and gave away his lunch money, all the while enduring the slurs that the bully dished out with the blows.

Misconceptions about global geography have been exacerbated by the demise of geography in educational systems. When geography became marginalized in the education system in the United States, the trend spread like wildfire throughout the world education systems (Barrs 1988). We remember the days when in elementary school, students learned everything about every country on Earth that was already mapped. However, when later generations went to school, the curriculum, class texts, and the atlas had changed so much that one could barely recognize the information they contained when compared to earlier versions. Local geography became not about the students' own country, but about their village and county.

Although world systems theorists and historians are moving away from frameworks centered on continental landmasses and ideological power toward a more unified and broader conceptualization of the continents grounded in a critical analysis of spaces, mapping, and naming practices, it does not erase the fact that Africa remains tied to the labels that outsiders imposed (Ozias and Pasque 2017). Today more than ever, even as Africans search for their own identities, we wonder what would be the most appropriate ways to categorize the continents in the twenty-first century, in the era of increased globalization, interlocking politico-economic zones, when we face issues of deglobalization, protectionism, and global capitalism that feel bereft of concern for populations at large and lacking in ethics and morality, with the continuing health, economic, and environmental effects of the recent COVID-19 crisis. Is the scramble for Africa as a strategy of *veni, vidi, vici*, "I came, I saw, I conquered," over yet?

Hierarchical conceptions of global geography, such as "First, Second, and Third Worlds," and the expression of complex spatial phenomena in simplistic (and often incorrect) concepts, such as Black and White, are examples of bigoted global cartography. Such a practice "does injustice to the complexities of

4 SUB-SAHARAN AFRICAN IMMIGRANTS' STORIES

global geography," as does the idea that "cultural identities (nations) coincide with politically sovereign entities" (Lewis and Wigen 2019, 1–8). Where the continents lay is of no significance. More important is their relative ranking. Ill-meaning and Eurocentric cartographers use geographical concepts and global cartography to influence human imagination about the various areas of the globe. The result is that some landmasses are given undue significance while influencing international politics and economic policies. This is why power brokers divide and categorize the world into continents with the West being the highest-order geographical concept, signifying better, if not the best, and a wealthy Global North is juxtaposed with a Global South, with little regard for how that wealth was acquired or where it came from.

Africa has had many nicknames since colonizers "discovered" her, including the land of Ham/dark skins, the Garden of Eden, Mother Continent, Motherland, dark or black continent, Kingdom in the Sky, and the land of Cush/Kush, as well as mother of mankind and Cradle of Humankind. There are many theories as to the origin of its current name. The oldest written evidence derives from the ancient Egyptian language that described their land as provided by the Nile River. Kemet, one of the ancient Egyptian words for their land, means black soil or people from the black soil, associating the people living there with the soil that the Nile brought north with every flood.

The great African historian, Cheikh Anta Diop, in his extensive research and two-cradle theory, illustrated key underlying structures and foundations of African cultures. In his book *Kemetic History of Afrika*, Cheikh Anta Diop (1991) writes that the ancient name of Africa, Alkebulan, came into use in the late seventeenth century and was given to the continent by the ancient Greeks and Romans (Diop 1991). It is the oldest and only word of indigenous origin that was used by the Moors, Nubians, Numidians, Khart-Haddans (Carthagenians), and Ethiopians, to mean "mother of mankind" or "Garden of Eden" (Diop 1991).

We did a little search using public data sources like Google and Wikipedia: One theory holds that the name Africa is derived from the Roman designation of the area as Afri, after the name of a Berber tribe that Romans had encountered. Another theory suggests that the modern word comes from Aprica, which means sunny or dusty, maybe in reference to the Sahara Desert. The term Guiné or Guinea was used by European colonizers to describe part of West Africa. Thus far we can see that the interior of Africa had not yet been visited or "discovered," and so most Europeans did not know what peoples and riches were there.

A third theory posits that the name African comes from the Greek word Aphrike, meaning a land without cold or horror. In modern times, up through the early twentieth century, Western sources called the southern Nile valley Aethiopia, following ancient Greek sources that referred to that area by that name, meaning the land of the dark-skinned or burnt peoples. One possibility is that the name Africa was bestowed by traders from India who referred to the continent as Apara, meaning "west of," maybe from the perspective of their own land.

Additionally, another theory from the sixteenth century is associated with two people: a famous medieval traveler and scholar named Leo Africanus (al-Hasan ibn Muhammad al-Wazzan) and a Chief or Warlord whose name was not given. It is believed that the continent got its name from Leo Africanus. His travel records indicated a good understanding of the northern part of the continent, just like every other theory discussed earlier and is said to have influenced the choice of the name Africa for the continent. Yet another theory associated with the Phoenicians labeled the continent as the land of corn and fruits.

As a result of centuries of global internalization of negative images and stereotypes of Africa and its people and cultures, there is great resistance to understanding Africa as a richly diverse continent, with a multitude of histories, cultures, languages, and environments. Wole Soyinka (2012, 27) points out the fact that Africa has not suffered under a "discovery" narrative, as many other lands have done: "Africa appears to have been 'known about' speculated over, explored both in actuality and fantasy, even mapped—Greeks, Jews, Arabs, Phoenicians, etc., took turns—but no narrative has come down to us that actually lays personal or racial claim to the discovery of the continent. Ancient ruins, the source of a river, mountain peaks, exotic kingdom, and sunken pyramids, yes, but not the continent itself—as in the case of the Americas."

This discourse on naming and the power to name is the subtext behind the terms used throughout this work. As researchers, we use the term sub-Saharan African immigrants—despite the fact that it is not a term we would use to describe ourselves—because it is a term commonly used by others to refer to us and our place of origin. We are also part of the migration patterns we are discussing, including the historical Bantu migration and the trade in enslaved Africans that is often and incorrectly used as the sole criterion to describe and define the cultural geography of the African continent. Currently, Africa has more internally displaced people than any other continent, whether through forced or voluntary immigration. Many of these displaced people, like us, are highly educated and come from highly educated African countries.

Many immigrants from sub-Saharan Africa consider emigration to the West as an opportunity for educational and economic self-fulfillment. But their reality is too often that their needs and interests along with their skills and talents remain poorly understood and underutilized because most countries do not recognize their presence and do little to facilitate their integration. Moreover, only a few studies on immigration to the United States have specifically mentioned the impact of African immigration (Butcher 1994; Obenga 1996; Dodoo 1997; Arthur 2000; Kent 2007; Massey et al. 2007; Arthur 2008; Uzoigwe 2008; Chothia 2013; wa Muiu 2013; Smith 2014; Anderson 2017; Echeverria-Estrada and Batalova 2019; Ndlovu-Gatsheni 2019; Oliphant 2019; US Census Bureau 2019).

We are undertaking this book project to investigate the phenomenon of immigration of sub-Saharan Africans in the West and to tell our own personal stories and to share our lived experiences of perseverance, our survival and coping strategies, and our continued experience with discounting and devaluing. In doing so, we hope that future generations of African immigrants can learn from and be encouraged by our resilience, resistance, and successes, and realize that their experiences are not unique and that the obstacles they will encounter are not insurmountable (hooks 1989). Among the stories and issues, we present are how immigrants reconcile their understanding of success from their respective worldviews with the meaning of success in the countries they have emigrated to; how emigration has affected their personal, academic, social, cultural, economic, and professional lives; and finally, what mechanisms of resistance they have developed to adapt to their new contexts.

The gap that currently exists in the social sciences literature—a gap that this research begins to fill—is that little to no work has been devoted to understanding the distinctive experiences of sub-Saharan African immigrants. In addition, little research exists about the multifaceted problems of integration and assimilation to Western societies that sub-Saharan African immigrants encounter, the complexity of the process of transplantation and most importantly, the different strategies of survival they have developed to cope with the new challenges they face in their respective host countries.

Immigration policies in the West do not generally address the peculiar circumstances of sub-Saharan Africans who are in the Western countries legally. For example, the Comprehensive Immigration Reform in the United States focuses only on border security and other immigrant punitive measures including worksite enforcement penalties and employment eligibility verification, but the policy does nothing to support immigrants from Africa. Throughout the literature and government census reports that were reviewed for this project, the recurring finding was that immigrants from Africa were the most rapidly growing and highly educated population of Black immigrants from sub-Saharan Africa, and that trend is expected to increase (Kent 2007). Furthermore, many African immigrants are highly educated, with nearly 65 percent of them having one or more years of college education

(*The Journal of Blacks in Higher Education*, 1999, 26: 60–61.). Yet, many of them are underemployed. By comparison, as of 2019, approximately 30 percent of the entire American population, aged 25 years or older, has a bachelor's degree or equivalent (US Census Bureau 2019).

Purpose of the Book

For the purposes of this book, the concept of sub-Saharan African immigration to the United States refers to immigrants who are or were nationals of countries in so-called sub-Saharan Africa and who are now in the United States as students, lawful permanent residents, or citizens. This group of immigrants in the United States is the nation's most highly educated, as briefly discussed earlier and in detail later. The purpose of this research is to give a voice to just a few of the countless stories of the personal lived experiences of sub-Saharan African immigrants in the West.

Our goal for this phenomenological study is to provide a unique forum where the voices of the sub-Saharan African immigrants can be heard as they tell their authentic stories to serve as a record for future immigrants. This study will also give them an opportunity to see how powerful, liberating, and valuable their stories and experiences are, not only for them but also for others. This validation of one another's experiences demonstrates that one is never alone and that one's experiences are never necessarily isolated. There are many factors and perspectives that affect them.

Indeed, understanding the specific experiences of sub-Saharan Africans in the West could be of tremendous benefits to newly arriving immigrants. Thus, this book seeks to produce a more specific description of sub-Saharan African immigration in the United States by recording our reflections, experiences, and strategies of coping, as well as those of the participants. We hope that the insights gained from the research in this book will be used by immigrant communities, academic institutions, and governmental agencies in advocating for immigration policies that positively impact the lived experiences of sub-Saharan African immigrants, and in planning support interventions.

What makes this book unique is that the personal narratives and lived experiences of the authors themselves are included in the study that guided the discussions. We recognize and elaborate on the methodological challenges that our role as researcher-participants pose to our research project. However, we believe that telling our own stories from our own perspectives is important and empowering because when others tell our stories there are omissions, misrepresentations, and stereotypes. It is this dissatisfaction with the way our experiences and ways of sense-making are misrepresented that motivated us to write this book from a phenomenological and researcher-participant approach. We believe that our experiences not only as sub-Saharan African immigrants, but also as researcher-participants are as valuable and valid.

Furthermore, our experiences increase our credibility as scholars and researchers. In this book, we undertake to give immigrants a space and platform as well as a voice to portray and share their personal stories, in their own terms to humanize them. By humanizing them through their personal stories, we hope to underscore the fact that their experiences and their uniqueness could be the stories of any other American, as they have the same aspirations, dreams, and hopes that many Americans have. As such, we wish to delineate our sameness as human beings. We provide ideas for researchers, policymakers, academic institutions, and governments to better meet sub-Saharan immigrants' needs in terms of support and interventions, teaching and learning needs, as well as needs related to their smooth transition into society.

The authors' ability to tell our stories alongside our participants' stories gives us an opportunity to share our experiences freely even as we learn together. This can also help other sub-Saharan immigrants avoid some of the pitfalls and challenges that some of us have endured because we did not have such support from those who came before us. Somolu (2007) states that story sharing can help communities of immigrants by providing support and information about resources that are available to them as they adapt to the new environment. Somolu further asserts that story sharing may also provide immigrants with a safe space to process the strong emotions that might arise from their reflections as they relive their experiences and tell their stories.

The authors are focusing on a specific although broad geographical part of Africa (see the definition above from the United Nations and the IMF) to avoid portraying African immigrants as a monolithic group. Sub-Saharan African immigrants who reside in the United States are from many different countries and backgrounds, and it is important that we continue to explore their lived experiences in its diversity.

Implications and Significance of the Study

This research is intended to be a record for future immigrants on coping and survival mechanisms, and it could also be used by the United States to plan support interventions. A better understanding of the specific experiences of sub-Saharan Africans in the West could help host countries develop better social programs to serve the needs of those immigrants and ensure their smooth transition and integration. Most immigrants contribute to the gross domestic product of their home countries through remittances and support they give to their families back home. We expect that this research would also give African countries of origin the opportunity to use the information here to plan for incentive programs and investment opportunities where African immigrants can invest and meaningfully contribute to the economic development of their respective countries of origin.

Our perspective as sub-Saharan African immigrants adds to the complexities of immigration in the United States. We present stories that document the struggles of maintaining jobs, going to college, sustaining and maintaining relationships, and providing for ourselves in a way that brings us joy in what we do. The differences here show up through the individual stories. African immigrants who reside in the United States are from many different backgrounds, and it is important that we continue to explore what this diversity means in its entirety. Regardless of our socioeconomic status, nationality, ethnicity, race, or gender, our status as immigrants connects us, as we all know what it feels like to be labeled as the "other." We all know what it feels like to be marginalized, devalued, and discounted because of our very presence in this country.

Literature Review

It is our stories that connect us. It is our stories that allow us to hold up the mirror that looks like somebody else's life, but we actually get to see ourselves.
—Oprah Winfrey

This section of the book presents literature that was reviewed during the research process. The strategy used was a content review of books and peer-reviewed journal articles, relevant literature, and government documents. The analyzed and synthesized information is presented in the upcoming chapters according to the recurring themes that emerged, including where sub-Saharan African immigrants come from, their cultural values, where they settle in the United States, and the challenges experienced, education attainment and jobs, immigration trends, pull and push factors, coping strategies, relationships, health issues, the dreams of succeeding, and the myth of going back home. When the authors started this project in 2014, there was hardly any literature on sub-Saharan African immigrants and their lived experience in the United States. As of 2021, there has been an increase in such studies, and we present a discussion in this section that is richer because of that.

The United States Immigration and Nationality Act of 1952 defines the term immigrant as every alien. An alien is defined as any person who is not a citizen or national of the United States, except those legally admitted under nonimmigrant categories. A refugee is a particular type of alien, someone unable or unwilling to return to their country of nationality for reasons of personal safety, who may have their status legally adjusted. As detailed in government documents, immigrants from Africa constitute a highly diverse, educated, and rapidly growing group in the United States (*The Journal of Blacks in Higher Education* 26: 60–61). The African foreign-born population reportedly doubled in size between 2000 and 2010 (US Census Bureau 2011).

The flow of African immigration to the United States was less in the early decades of the 1960s and 1970s immediately following the independence of most African countries. However, that trend dramatically reversed in the 1980s and 1990s. The number of African immigrants who came to the United States between 1982 and 1992 grew by about 500 times the number of African immigrants who arrived in the United States between 1861 and 1961 (Takyi and Konadu-Agyemang 2006). The rate of sub-Saharan African immigration to the United States has drastically increased since the 2000s (Capps et al. 2012; Oliphant 2019) with the steady increase attributed to the Diversity Visa program of 1990, refugee movements, and family reunification strategies and policies in the United States (Thomas 2011).

According to data on African migration to the United States synthesized from the Department of Homeland Security 2018 Yearbook, Migration Policy Institute, the Pew Research Center, and the New American Economy, most immigrants (45 percent) came to the United States because they were immediate relatives of US citizens, while others came as refugees and asylees (22 percent), on diversity visas (18 percent), as members of the extended family of US citizens (10 percent), and via employment-based preferences (4 percent) (Department of Homeland Security 2018). Although the Diversity Visa lottery looks like it has a low percentage, it accounts for higher economic return to the United States. This visa category requires immigration from countries with historically low rates of immigration to the United States, and all applicants are required to have at least a high school diploma or a minimum of two years of experience working in a field that requires two or more years of vocational training. The lottery thus gives preference to immigrants with relatively high levels of education and transferable skill sets. Typically, those types of people are able to bear the economic burden of migrating and sustaining themselves after arrival in the United States without incurring public charge.

Previous scholarship on African emigration to the United States often explores the evolution, push and pull factors, trends of African migration, and skills of African immigrants to the United States, especially from postcolonial times well into the first and a half decade of the twenty-first century (Massey 1998; Hoggart and Mendoza 1999; Owusu 1999; Arthur 2000; Hatton and Williamson 2003; Adepoju 2004, 2006; Eastwood et al. 2005; Hagopian et al. 2005; Carling 2011). As noted earlier, 30 percent of the entire American population that is 25 years or older has a bachelor's degree (US Census Bureau 2019). The same report indicates that 48.9 percent of sub-Saharan African immigrants hold a college degree, a rate that was more than double that of native-born White Americans, and almost four times the rate of native-born African Americans. The highest rate was that of Egyptian Americans at 59.7 percent, followed by Nigerian Americans at 58.6 percent.

The 48.9 percent of college-educated sub-Saharan Africans includes some PhD holders who are college professors and researchers. Other sub-Saharan African immigrants are gainfully employed in management, business, science, and the arts (37 percent); service occupations (25 percent); production, transportation, and material moving occupations (18 percent); sales and office work (17 percent); and natural resources, construction, and maintenance (3 percent) (Chishti et al. 2017).

Tererai Trent, PhD, is a recent example of the many sub-Saharan African immigrants who come to the United States to study and then return to their countries of origin to improve the livelihoods of their communities. Trent appeared on *The Oprah Winfrey Show* in 2009 after earning her doctorate from Western Michigan University and being honored with a bronze "Statue of Equality" in New York for her education efforts through her Tererai Trent Foundation in Zimbabwe. In 1999, Ahmed Hassan Zewail, an Egyptian-American immigrant to the United States, won the Nobel Prize in chemistry for his work in femtochemistry. He received many other awards, but sadly died in 2016 at age 70.

We share these stories because discussions of African immigration in the United States, particularly in conjunction with globalization and the socioeconomic situation in many African countries, tend to focus on discourses around poverty, violence, displacement, and poor governance, rather than on topics such as Africans' aspirations and abilities to emigrate, the rate of African immigrants in the United States, and the uniqueness of African immigrants (Lugalla 1997; Hatton and Williamson 2003; Kent 2007; Wilson and Habecker 2008; Flahaux and De Haas 2016). Given previous discourses surrounding trends, rates, patterns, and drivers of African immigration to the United States, our work seeks to shift the focus away from statistical theories that tend to quantify and objectify African immigrants in the United States and toward creating a counternarrative and a counterculture to exert more agency over our lives as immigrants.

Terminologies Used in the Study

Safe space (termed by some scholars as a "brave space"): An environment where members of a social informal circle can share their stories and experiences freely and get support and validation from the other members. It is also a place where one feels free to express strong emotions without being judged or misunderstood.

Sub-Saharan Immigrants: Although there is a controversy about the use of the term "sub-Saharan" as being Eurocentric, the authors use it in this book to refer to African immigrants who are geographically from the region described as south of the Sahara Desert. These groups immigrated to the United States voluntarily, as opposed to those of African descent who were involuntarily brought to the United States by means of the historic Atlantic slave trade. Their primary purpose in immigrating was to seek educational or economic opportunities. The term African in the scope of this book refers to geographical or national origins rather than racial affiliation.

Major themes that emerged from the results of the study guided the structure of this book. They include issues of identity and what it means to be African; perspectives on success, racism and discrimination; coping and assimilation; silencing and denial issues; the myth of going back home; acculturation and the challenges of living in two worlds; accents and identity issues; cultural and value shift; and leadership issues.

The content of this book is mostly based on research conducted on sub-Saharan African immigrants in the United States. Most of these people considered emigration to the West as an opportunity for education. Education in most countries is still considered a ticket to good jobs and increased economic mobility. Indeed, most of the participants in the research for this book cited education as the main reason why they came to the United States. Others came with the hope of getting jobs in the United States or back in their native countries; to make money after graduation to live a good life and to support their families back home; and to join family and/or their spouses.

References

Adepoju, Aderanti. 2004. *Changing Configurations of Migration in Africa*. Migration Policy Institute.

Adepoju, Aderanti. 2006. "Recent Trends in International Migration in and from Africa." *Human Resources Development Centre*, Abuja, Nigeria.

Anderson, Monica. 2017. "African Immigrant Population in U.S. Steadily Climbs." *Pew Research Center*, February 14, 2017. www.pewresearch.org/fact-tank/2017/02/14/african-immigrant-population-in-u-s-steadily-climbs.

Arthur, John A. 2000. *Invisible Sojourners: African Immigrant Diaspora in the United States*. Westport, CT: Praeger Publishers.

Arthur, John A. 2008. *The African Diaspora in the United States and Europe: A Ghanaian Experience*. Burlington, VT: Ashgate.

Barrs, David. 1988. "School Geography in the USA." *Teaching Geography* 13, no. 1: 4–6.

Brown, Keith, and Sarah Ogilvie. 2010. *Concise Encyclopedia of Languages of the World.* Oxford, UK: Elsevier.

Butcher, Kristin F. 1994. "Black Immigrants in the United States: A Comparison with Native Blacks and Other Immigrants." *ILR Review* 47, no. 2: 265–84.

Capps, Randy, Kristen McCabe, and Michael Fix. 2012. "Diverse Streams: African Migration to the United States." *Migration Policy Institute.* www.migrationpolicy.org/research/cbi-african-migration-united-states.

Carling, Jørgen. 2011. "The European Paradox of Unwanted Immigration." In *A Threat against Europe*, edited by J. Peters Burgess and Serge Gutwirth, 33–46. Brussels University Press (VUB) Press.:.

Chishti, M., Pierce, S. and Bolter, J. 2017. Migration Policy Institute. Washington, DC.

Chothia, Farouk. 2013. "How Welcome Are Africans in the UK?" *BBC World.* November 27, 2013. www.bbc.com/news/world-africa-25111177.

Department of Homeland Security. 2018. *Yearbook of Immigration Statistics 2018.* www.dhs.gov/immigration-statistics/yearbook/2018.

Diop, Cheikh Anta. 1991. *Civilization or Barbarism.* Chicago: Lawrence Hill Books .

Dodoo, F. Nii-Amoo. 1997. "Assimilation Differences among Africans in America." *Social Forces* 76, no. 2: 527–46.

Eastwood, John B., Rachel E. Conroy, Sarala Naicker, Peter A. West, Roger C. Tutt, and Jacob Plange-Rhule. 2005. "Loss of Health Professionals from Sub-Saharan Africa: The Pivotal Role of the UK." *The Lancet* 365, no. 9474: 1893–1900.

Echeverria-Estrada, Carlos and Jeanne Batalova. 2019. *Sub-Saharan African Immigrants in the United States.* https://www.migrationpolicy.org/article/sub-saharan-african-immigrants-united-states-2018#Distribution.

Flahaux, Marie-Laurence, and Hein De Haas. 2016. "African Migration: Trends, Patterns, Drivers." *Comparative Migration Studies* 4, no. 1: 1–25.

Gall, Rev. James. 1885. "Use of Cylindrical Projections for Geographical Astronomical, and Scientific Purposes." *Scottish Geographical Magazine* 1, no. 4: 119–23. doi: 10.1080/14702548508553829.

Hagopian, Amy, Anthony Ofosu, Adesegun Fatusi, Richard Biritwum, Ama Essel, L. Gary Hart, and Carolyn Watts. 2005. "The Flight of Physicians from West Africa: Views of African Physicians and Implications for Policy." *Social Science & Medicine* 61, no. 8: 1750–60.

Hatton, Timothy J., and Jeffrey G. Williamson. 2003. "Demographic and Economic Pressure on Emigration Out of Africa." *The Scandinavian Journal of Economics* 105, no. 3: 465–86.

Hoggart, Keith, and Cristóbal Mendoza. 1999. "African Immigrant Workers in Spanish Agriculture." *Sociologia Ruralis* 39, no. 4: 538–62.

Hooks, Bell. 1989. *Talking Back: Thinking Feminist, Thinking Black.* Vol. 10. Boston: South End Press.

Kent, Mary. 2007. "Immigration and America's Black Population." *Population Bulletin* 62, no. 4: 5–17.

Khapoya, Vincent B. 2013. *The African Experience: An Introduction.* New York: Routledge.

Lewis, Martin W., and Kären Wigen. 1997. *The Myth of Continents: A Critique of Metageograpgy.* Berkeley: University of California Press.

Lugalla, Joe. 1997. "Economic Reforms and Health Conditions of the Urban Poor in Tanzania." *African Studies Quarterly* 1, no. 2: 19.

Massey, D. S. (Ed.). 1998. *Worlds in Motion: Understanding International Migration at the End of the Millennium.* Oxford: Oxford University Press.

Massey, Douglas S. 2007. *Categorically Unequal: The American Stratification System.* New York: Russell Sage Foundation.

Nicol, Davidson S. H. W., John Innes Clarke, Robert K. A. Gardiner, David N. McMaster, Kwamina Busumafi Dickson, Robert Walter Steel, Alfred Kröner, John F. M. Middleton, Audrey Smedley, and Akinlawon Ladipo Mabogunje. 2021. "Africa." *Encyclopedia Britannica.* September 28, 2021. Accessed June 6, 2022. www.britannica.com/place/Africa.

Ndlovu-Gatsheni, S. J. 2019. "Discourses of decolonization/decoloniality." *Papers on Language and Literature,* 55, no. 3: 201–26.

Obenga, T. 1996. "Nubia and Its Relationship with Egypt (1780–1700)." In *History of Humanity: Scientific and Cultural Development, Volume II: From the Third Millennium to the Seventh Century BC,* edited by A. H. Dani, et al., 372–88. New York: Routledge.

Oliphant, Sarah Moore. 2019. "Voices of Ethiopian Immigrant Women." *International Social Work* 62, no. 2: 581–94.

Owusu, Thomas Y. 1999. "Residential Patterns and Housing Choices of Ghanaian Immigrants in Toronto, Canada." *Housing Studies* 14, no. 1: 77–97.

Owusu, Thomas Y. 2003. "Transnationalism among African Immigrants in North America: The Case of Ghanaians in Canada." *Journal of International Migration and Integration/Revue de l'integration et de la migration internationale* 4, no. 3: 395–413.

Ozias, Moira, and Penny Pasque. 2017. "Critical Geography as Theory and Praxis: The Community–University Imperative for Social Change." *The Journal of Higher Education* 90, no. 1: 85–110. doi: 10.1080/00221546.2018.1449082.

Smith, Amy Elizabeth. 2014. "The Lived Experience of Black African Nurses Educated within the United States." UNLV Theses/Dissertations/Professional Papers/Capstones. Paper 2144. digitalscholarship.unlv.edu/cgi/viewcontent.cgi?article=3145&context=thesesdissertations.

Somolu, O. 2007. "Telling our own stories': African women blogging for social change." In *Women Worldwide: Transnational Feminist Perspectives on Women,* edited by J. Lee and S. M. Shaw, 102–8. New York: McGraw-Hill.

Soyinka, W., 2012. *Of Africa.* New Haven: Yale University Press.

Takyi, Baffour K., and Kwadwo Konadu-Agyemang. 2006. "Theoretical Perspectives on African Migration." In *The New African Diaspora in North America,* edited by Kwadwo Konadu-Agyemang, Baffour K. Takyi, and John A. Arthur, 13–16. New York: Lexington Books.

Thomas, K. J. 2011. "What Explains the Increasing Trend in African Emigration to the US?" *International Migration Review,* 45, no. 1: 3–28.

UN Security Council. 2020. "International Organisation of la Francophonie Plays Vital Role in Peacebuilding, Assistant Secretary-General Tells Security Council." Press Release, September 8, 2020. https://www.un.org/press/en/2020/sc14295.doc.htm.

UNEP-WCMC. 2016. *The State of Biodiversity in Africa: A Mid-term Review of Progress towards the Aichi Biodiversity Targets.* Cambridge, UK: United Nations Environment Programme World Conservation Monitoring Centre (UNEP-WCMC).

US Census Bureau. 2011. American Community Survey. American FactFinder. https://data.census.gov/cedsci/.

US Census Bureau. 2019. *Foreign-born-population from Africa.*

Uzoigwe, Godfrey. 2008. "A Matter of Identity: Africa and Its Diaspora in America since 1900, Continuity and Change." *African and Asian Studies* 7, no. 2–3: 259–88.

wa Muiu, Mueni. 2013. "African Countries' Political Independence at Fifty: In Search of Democracy, Peace and Social Justice." *African and Asian Studies* 12, no. 4: 331–51.

Wilson, Jill H., and Shelly Habecker. 2008. "The Lure of the Capital City: An Anthrogeographical Analysis of Recent African Immigration to Washington, DC." *Population, Space and Place* 14, no. 5: 433–48.

Windley, Brian Frederick. 2020. "Precambrian." *Encyclopedia Britannica*. March 21, 2020. Accessed June 6, 2022. www.britannica.com/science/Precambrian.

Chapter 2

METHODOLOGY: A PHENOMENOLOGICAL STUDY OF SUB-SAHARAN AFRICAN IMMIGRANTS

Many stories matter. Stories have been used to dispossess and to malign. But stories can also be used to empower, and to humanize. Stories can break the dignity of a people. But stories can also repair that broken dignity.
— Adichie, 2009 TEDGlobal

In this chapter, the authors discuss the challenges of using phenomenology as a research design, where the researcher is also a participant or has similar characteristics as the subjects of the research. This calls for the researcher to become a researcher-participant, which comes with its own challenges, including maintaining unbiased interconnection between the authors as researchers and as the object of research (researcher-participants), and still being able to give a voice to nameless and countless stories that represent the personal experiences of sub-Saharan African immigrants in the United States. Research data is great, but stories from and by engaged respondents living the phenomena being investigated are more inspiring and actionable. Involved knowing and lived experiences, combined with rigorous research methodology, is in itself a researcher's challenge.

The authors were in every step of the research cognizant of the fact that personal knowing rather than objective, methodological knowledge was crucial to the authenticity of the results because of being directly and personally involved in what we know by lived experiences about the phenomenon. This personal dimension of knowing through experience is an advantage in that it opens up and expands the phenomena that is being studied and also in the course of interpreting it.

We chose to use qualitative inquiry as our guiding methodological approach because it involves "the studied use and collection of a variety of empirical materials [...] that describe routine and problematic moments and meanings in people's lives" (Denzin and Lincoln 1994, 2) as well as "the nature and meaning of things, a phenomenon's essence and essentials that determine what it is" (Saldana 2011, 7). Qualitative inquiry allowed us to examine the meaning-making process and the resulting meaning made by sub-Saharan African immigrants about their lived experiences as they made decisions to emigrate. Further, it allowed us to explore their experiences as they navigated their new environment in the places they choose to settle once in the United States and the impact it had on their lives (Van Manen 1990; Moustakas 1994; Hein and Austin 2001; Giorgio 2009). The phenomenon that our research explores is the stories of sub-Saharan African immigrants in the United States. More precisely, we used a hermeneutic phenomenological approach, which offers a more descriptive, reflective, and interpretive mode of inquiry regarding an individual's description of their experiences in the world (Van Manen 1990).

Background Information

Being faced with the reality of what it means to be Black in America and other European countries for the first time in their lives can lead to serious physical as well as mental issues for immigrants. Several research findings have documented not only the negative impact of racial stereotyping and discrimination on the mental health of Blacks, but have also drawn a parallel between African immigrants' ability to develop a transnational identity (racial, ethnic, and that of host country) and their desire to successfully confront racism and discrimination (Redway 2014).

As mentioned earlier, immigration policies in the United States are largely punitive, and they lack any type of support structure for immigrants who have entered the country through formal channels. In the UK, immigration reform and new policies are not only harsh, they are viewed as racist (Green 2015). Although The British Nationality Act 1948 granted the subjects of the British Empire the right to live and work in the UK, recent years have seen tighter immigration controls implemented even on Commonwealth citizens (Somerville et al. 2009; Chothia 2013).

Throughout the literature and government census reports that were reviewed for this project, the recurring finding was that immigrants from Africa were the most rapidly growing and highly educated population of Black immigrants from sub-Saharan Africa and that number is expected to continue to increase (Kent 2007). It was further reported that many of them are highly educated, underemployed, yet nearly 65 percent of African immigrants have one or more years of college education. This in comparison to records of the US Census Bureau that indicate that about 30 percent of the entire American population that is 25 years or older has a bachelor's degree or equivalent.

The majority of the Black immigrants from sub-Saharan Africa came from Nigeria, Kenya, Ethiopia, Ghana, and South Africa, and recently more are coming in from Somalia and Sudan. African immigrants now make up 1.6 million or 36 percent of the Black immigrant population (Pew Research Center 2013; US Census Bureau 2019). However, their needs and interests along with their skills and talents remain poorly understood and underutilized with most states in the United States and European countries barely recognizing their presence and doing little to facilitate their integration.

Purpose of Study

The purpose of this chapter is to reflect on and discuss the challenges of using phenomenology as a research design and maintaining unbiased interconnection between us as researchers and as the object of research. As mentioned earlier, using phenomenology as a design, we tell stories and present some of the issues of how sub-Saharan immigrants reconcile their understanding of success from their respective worldviews with the meaning of success in the countries they have emigrated to; how emigration has affected their personal, academic, social, economic, and professional lives; and what mechanisms of resistance they have developed in order to adapt to their new context.

In this chapter and the whole book, the term sub-Saharan African immigrants in the United States refers to nationals of Africa who are not North Africans, but from the region commonly referred to as sub-Sahara.

Researcher Bias

Another major challenge that the authors faced while using phenomenology as a research design was bracketing to avoid bias. As we describe below, bracketing allows researchers to focus on the "phenomena," or the experiences, thoughts, and emotions—all the things that happen in the mind—without applying judgment to them. Although in this book we the authors are researchers, we are not very different from the participants in terms of place of origin, race, gender, and education as well as some minority characteristics such as ethnicity and social economic class. Our reasons for coming to the United States are also not very different: education, family reunification, and economic uplifting. The researchers are Black women who have experienced the challenges of leaving their home countries and being immigrants in the United States where racial bias especially about Black people is real and continues to hamper the development of that minoritized group.

The research on lived experiences that we share here was done with the aim of getting a deeper understanding of the phenomena for personal self-change, to get a chance to tell our own stories, for use in the future as life and student coaches in our roles as professors in higher education institutions, and most importantly to give the current and future immigrants a voice and validation about their experiences.

Limitations

Phenomenological research generates a large quantity of interview notes and audio recordings. Transcribing and describing the experiences and yet keeping the meaning as close to the original was daunting. We made the best attempt. One other limitation we wish to note is that we did not explicitly explore the question about the silence and denials of issues we sensed they did not want to talk about or that we were aware happens often in Africa but participants did not feel free to bring it up unless probed.

Protection of Human Participants

The goal of this descriptive phenomenological study is to get a deeper and richer understanding of sub-Saharan African immigrants' experiences in the United States. Participants were allowed control over what and how much information to share and their voice was maintained as much as possible. The researchers were keenly on the lookout for paralanguage and indications of willful omissions or distortions and clarified these with follow-up questions. The study was conducted after being approved by Western Michigan University Institutional Review Board. When the research questionnaire was ready and the researchers had addressed the Protection of Human Subjects issues to the best of their knowledge, the researchers met to review that they had taken all precautions and required training on ethical research so as to ensure respect and no harm to the human subjects in this research.

During the process of recruiting participants, individuals were informed of this voluntary study, the purpose and the procedures and the benefits of participating as well as the strict confidentiality and freedom from harm with which the research would be conducted. Respondents were also informed of the freedom to ask questions at any point of the interview process and freedom to withdraw whenever they choose without any obligation or explanation as to their reasons for withdrawing from the study. There was no requirement to complete an exit interview or to cooperate with follow-up activities.

Research Methodology, Design and Procedures

The primary objective of this phenomenological study was to explicate the meaning, structure, and essence of the lived experiences of sub-Saharan African immigrants. This chapter presents data coding and analysis process and the critical themes that emerged. Participants were interviewed using structured and unstructured questions, which guided their description of their lived phenomenal experiences (see Appendix 1). The interactive process was used to gather data through in-depth interviews and detailed descriptions of their experiences, some of which were recorded digitally and others through written self-reports.

The researchers' aim was not to produce a general description of how to conduct a phenomenological study, but to record the challenges we faced during the process, our reflection, experiences and strategies of coping, as well as those of the respondents for future immigrants, communities, and governments to use in planning support interventions. Understanding the specific experiences of sub-Saharan African immigrants in the West could help Western host countries develop better social programs to serve the needs of those immigrants and ensure their smooth transition and integration.

By doing so, this book fills a gap in a much-needed literature and methodology about the lived experiences of the fastest growing immigrant populations in the West (US Census Bureau 2019). In the process of conducting this research, we found out that some of our respondents already had unstructured forums where they met and shared foods from their countries of origin. In addition to being therapeutic, the support circles that these immigrants have built have become their safe spaces for their members and we will be describing them as such. These would be a great opportunity for other researchers to expand research on this group. The researchers plan on tapping into it for a future coaching and mentoring program.

Many sub-Saharan African immigrants come to America and other European countries, completely unaware of the different ways in which racism and discrimination can negatively impact their lives and even derail their initial plans of achieving their education and/or economic dreams. Indeed, most of them initially believed that their hard work ethic will ultimately lead them to economic success and they completely discounted the impact of race on their lived experiences. Just to come to the realization of the insidious social and economic implications of race in America as well as other countries in the Global North (Chothia 2013) is a continuous challenge.

Being qualitative in nature, the phenomenological design enabled the researchers to explore and describe the lived experiences and sense-making process of sub-Saharan African Immigrants. To collect quality data, in-depth approaches including open-ended, unstructured questions and follow-up discussions were used. This was presented to the respondents as an evolving set of questions "that may seem more like a friendly conversation than a data-gathering interview" (Knox and Burkard 2009, 3). This in and of itself is a great challenge. The researchers had to constantly refocus themselves and bracket their experiences and emotions or else they would lose themselves in the story and emotions of empathy, and it would become intertwined with their own.

Bracketing had to be used consciously all the time to avoid bias where there was data that was outside the researchers' experience and/or expectation. On dealing with the recorded text and allowing for the phenomena to speak for itself, Moustakas (1994) advised researchers to ensure that the meaning, essence, and intention are understood. The next step was an intuitive reflective interpretation process so as not to overlook a person's individuality that came through the words and emotions as they narrated their stories. Phenomenology allows a researcher to gain a deeper understanding of the nature or meaning of the everyday experiences of the target audience because apart from being interactive, it is within the participants' environment.

Simms and Stawarska (2013) and Fisher and Embree (2000) offer that a researcher's role at this phase is to give participants an opportunity to voice their concerns and to share their lived experiences as a way to affirm their own efforts and agency in their success, with the understanding that knowledge and meaning is constructed individually and/or collaboratively. From the aggregated responses of 25 out the 30 sub-Saharan immigrants who completed our interview, the researchers were able to determine their perceptions on the impact of relocating to the United States and other countries, their coping strategies, and definition of success. Some of the participants revealed that they had relocated to countries like Malaysia before eventually ending up in the United States.

Once potential participants had been purposively recruited to take part in the research study, researchers engaged in a multiphasic informed consent process. The individual meeting served not only as the final phase of the informed consent process whereby potential participants could get any questions answered about the research as well as the interview session. During the first 15 minutes of the individual meeting, researchers finalized the informed consent process and obtained signatures and/or oral permission to proceed.

In the latter 45 minutes, researchers conducted the interview sessions and digitally recorded the responses for ease of transcription later on in the research process. The transcribing of the recorded contents of the entire interview of each participant was used to develop summaries of each interview. A hard copy of the transcribed interviews and summaries was stored in a locked file cabinet at one of the researchers' office at the university with no identifying information on them, thereby protecting the identity of the participants and upholding confidentiality.

These steps are very challenging when compared to quantitative research where the data-gathering tool is very impersonal and very anonymous; there is no content to record or transcribe because the goal is not maintaining the story and narration style, as is the case in phenomenological design. Once the interviews were transcribed, the researchers entered the data into qualitative data analysis software, which helped us develop codes and themes from the transcribed information. Researchers used the recurring themes from the responses to discuss and describe the inner and lived experiences of the participants. These themes form the chapters of this book.

Sample Size, Setting and Demographics

In phenomenological research, one cannot quite speak of sample size or representativeness. The participants in this research were purposively selected based on their shared experiences of being sub-Saharan African immigrants in the United States. Instead of the recommended six to eight, a purposive sample of 30 sub-Saharan Africans with experiences of the phenomena of study was selected. This sample was fundamental to the quality and trustworthiness of data and as such reliability and proximity to the respondents' experience had to be ensured. In addition, through completion of a short-structured questionnaire, the researchers collected quantitative data including age, gender, education level, as well as years lived in the United States.

The researchers' main task was to penetrate as deeply as possible into the respondents' world, so as to understand and describe their experience as completely as possible. Selecting subjects who offer an interesting, unusual, or particularly revealing set of circumstances as the selected sub-Saharan Africans for this study enabled the researchers to obtain comprehensive descriptions that provided the basis for a reflective structural analysis that portrayed the essences of the experience of being an immigrant from sub-Sahara Africa (Giorgi 2009).

Descriptive nominal statistics were used inductively to infer from the experience of being an immigrant in the United States. Internal validity issues for control included the subjective nature of personal narratives and inability to confirm the stories the respondents tell. To control for the likelihood of overstretching the subgroups in the research population that were more readily accessible, the researchers expanded the size to

30 instead of the recommended six to eight for phenomenological studies. The aim was to gather quality accounts and descriptions that were as vivid as possible bearing in mind that some respondents would be more articulate because of their clear perception about the phenomena being researched, while others would be hesitant to describe what they feel or what they are currently experiencing as it was still raw (Tables 2.1–2.7).

From a research perspective, all phenomenology is descriptive in the sense of aiming to describe rather than explain. However, the elements of reflection and interpretation seem to be embedded in the process of analyzing the responses, since the aim is to reveal essential general meaning structures of a phenomenon, while staying close to respondents' stories and meaning-making. This is done to avoid losing the richness and complexity of the descriptions of either the life world or lived experiences and to allow for "making assertions, which are supported by appropriate intuitive validations" (Giorgi, 2009) without judgment about the realness and meaningfulness of the phenomenon.

Since phenomenology is the study of experience as it is lived and structured through consciousness and not anecdotal (and beyond the dominant gaze), the accumulated evidence or knowledge is something that we "undergo" and also happens to us, and not something accumulated and mastered by us (Van Manen 1990). For the purpose of this book, hermeneutics as a study of experience and meaning through the process of interpretation and reinterpretation of meaning was adopted as an aid for interpretation and thus also of meaning by asking respondents to tell their story of lived experiences using unstructured and follow-up questions to focus them on the study.

Meaning in the context of this book, and based on the responses, became a basis for the researchers to continuously remain open to new insights and interpretations and further revisions as the conversations with the respondents progressed. For that reason, the ideal essences of experience or consciousness could not be isolated from the researchers' cultural and historical location.

Giorgi (2009) states four core characteristics that hold across all variations of phenomenological research: the research is rigorously descriptive, uses the phenomenological reductions, explores the intentional relationship between persons and situations, and discloses the essences, or structures, of meaning immanent in human experiences through the use of imaginative variation. Further, Giorgi (2009) argues that the phenomenological method encompasses three interlocking steps: (1) phenomenological reduction, (2) description, and (3) search for essences. Seidman's (1991) model, with its three-stage process, includes establishing the context of the respondents' experiences, constructing the experiences and reflecting on the meaning the experiences hold.

The following steps were included in the control measures: disclosing to the respondents the purpose of the study and how data would be used; avoiding leading questions but rather directing the respondents toward detailed description; withholding sharing personal impressions and speculative interpretation; not disclosing sensitive information; creating and following a realistic timeline; avoiding selection bias even though the study utilizes purposive inclusion/sampling; ensuring that important variables and their key elements were not overlooked; and bias or distortion of the conclusions was avoided.

The process of analyzing phenomenological data as suggested by Colaizzi (1978), Giorgi (2009), and Seidman (1991) was adopted as follows: identifying significant statements and phrases from the transcripts; formulating and aggregating meanings; categorizing, clustering, and integrating all the resulting ideas; describing the phenomenon exhaustively; creating a fundamental structure of the themes; and repeating the process for each respondent until saturation point is reached.

The following control measures as suggested by Creswell (2014, 201–3) were used at data analysis phase: triangulation of data sources to confirm that the research findings accurately reflect a person's, group's, or populous' observations; theoretical triangulation that involves the usage of more than one theoretical basis when interpreting collected data to add value to the triangulated data sources; avoiding siding with participants (going native) or disclosing only positive results; respecting the privacy of participants; reporting multiple perspectives and contrary findings; and developing composite/aggregate profiles.

The procedures discussed yielded data and insights that were significant to describe sub-Saharan African immigrants in the United States. The data was processed and analyzed using ATLAS.ti software to reveal frequencies and relationships, and also to describe the disparities. Thematic analysis of experiential accounts, theories, gestures, tones of voice, and pauses and other aspects of paralanguage, some feelings, emotions, and statements as well as a sufficient amount of the researchers' self-reflection, to uncover and clarify personal meaning, were also applied from an interpretive approach.

From the researchers' experience with this technique, the basic outcome of a phenomenology is the description of the meaning of a lived experience. The researchers acquired a deep understanding through the verbal reliving of the experience as expressed by the respondents. We made every attempt to be fully present and attentive and allowed respondents to give or narrate their lived experiences as a given. For aspects that the researchers felt the need for more clarity, through rephrasing and follow-up questions, they sought out further and deeper narrations. The reciprocal interactions between the researchers and respondents and their reflections brought out the narratives (Roulston 2010) that became the data set. This is the content that was categorized and analyzed.

To explicate and clarify implied meanings and to clarify answers, identify examples, generate information and themes, the interviewers used the method of rephrasing questions, engaging in critical discussions, and asking follow-up questions to get an in-depth narration of the situation. Meaning-making was done through the process of seeking clarification and examples, self-reflection, transcribing and intuitive thematic analysis of the field notes, and participants' feedback using a narrative analysis method and a descriptive phenomenological analysis independently from our own meaning-making and speculative interpretation. Before explication of the data or story analyses for common patterns, the researchers checked wording in the responses for clarity and shift in meaning and control for interviewer distortion and subversion by listening and rereading the scripts and transcribing carefully to avoid distortions and bias, incorrect inferences, and misinterpretations (Creswell 2014).

Collected data, or the whole texts after transcribing, was subjected to an inductive analysis and analyzed from an ontological approach by the researchers using an adapted version of an empirical phenomenological psychological method (Giorgi 2009). Significant and unique experiences were categorized and analyzed for differences and similarities. The results were further categorized into themes as shown in Table 2.8. This approach assisted in drawing out any hidden aspects within the narratives and in the interpreting process followed by describing them based on background understandings of sub-Saharan Africans and ourselves (Denzin 1989). ATLAS.ti software and its open, axial, and intuitive selective coding was used to label, transcribe, and closely review data before dividing it into major concepts and even smaller units or categories of meaning before identifying major recurrent stories or themes. Discriminant analysis was conducted using the five analytic steps outlined by Giorgi (2009) to identify patterns and organize and analyze themes (Figures 2.1–2.4).

To ensure we were following the above-discussed steps, we assumed the phenomenological attitude, listening to and reading and rereading the transcribed material. In the second step, we divided the transcribed data into meaning units or discernible parts that dealt with the aims of the study and the implications of the results rather than the lived meaning of the participants' experiences as we keenly read for a sense of the whole. In the third step and in the light of the whole interview, each meaning unit was condensed and transformed into codes. The fourth step, presented in the form of a synopsis after being synthesized, was the meaning units of the lived experiences of the respondents. In the fifth step, all the synopses from all the respondents were compared to find meaning structures that were recurring in all interviews.

The researchers ensured that the combined results reflected a careful description of precisely the features of the experienced phenomenon as they presented themselves to the consciousness of the researchers (Giorgi 2009). We undertook a thematic analysis involving searching through data to identify recurrent issues (Creswell 2014). We also engaged in the bracketing process as a way of creating an atmosphere and rapport for conducting the interview and setting aside personal emotions to enable objective pursuit of pure knowledge (Giorgi 2009). Bracketing the question and listening deeply while suspending any subjective perception of the bracketed question enabled the researchers to later examine and to analyze the meaning without judgment or imposition of our experience (Giorgi 2009); by conducting the interviews, researchers obtained descriptions of the experiences through methods such as informal interviewing, open-ended questions, and topical-guided interview.

Data Analysis: The Process

Setting and Demographics

Table 2.1 Participants' biodata

Age range	Total
19–22	2
23–26	2
27–30	4
31–33	3
34–37	1
38–41	0
42–45	3
46–49	3
50–53	1
54–57	2
57 and above	4

Table 2.2 Gender

Female	13
Male	12
Other	0

Table 2.3 Length of stay in the Unites States

Length range in years	Total
1 and below	0
2–5	3
6–9	5
10–13	3
14–17	3
18–21	5
22–25	1
26–29	2
29 and above	3

Table 2.4 Country of origin

Country	Total
Kenya	11
Ethiopia	2
Uganda	3
Rwanda	1
Burkina Faso	2
Senegal	1
Nigeria	3
Zambia	1
Botswana	1

Table 2.5 Reason for migrating

Reason	Total
Education	20
Marriage	3
Business	0
Family	2

Table 2.6 Education/degree achieved

None	2
Associate	0
Bachelors	12
Masters/MBA	6
PhD	4

Table 2.7 Marital status

Status	Total
Married	18
Single	7
Engaged	0
Living with girl/boyfriend	0

Participants' age ranged from 19 to over 65, but did not differ in terms of gender as shown in Table 2.1. Nonresponse rate was insignificant and did not affect the results. Further, being a phenomenology, each participant's story has its own level of significance and ability to give voice and validation to the individual. Education is the main reason why most of the African immigrants came to the Unites States as shown in Tables 2.5 and 2.6. Although most of them came when they were young and single, with time their status changed as indicated in Table 2.7.

Data Organization and Coding

Data was organized by transcribing the audios manually, listening again and again to confirm quality, compiling them all into one text document, and then uploading it to ATLAS.ti qualitative analysis software. This process enabled the identification and construction of frameworks guided by the research questions and the conceptual frameworks. The data was then sorted into the framework and labeled ready for descriptive analysis and later for discussing the relationships (Figures 2.1–2.4).

The main challenge was the reading and rereading a text, listening to the audios over and over, taking notes, reflecting on the data and writing down interpretations, and ensuring that none of the responses were omitted or misrepresented. Using ATLAS.ti qualitative data analysis software, the researchers used open coding to initially create as many codes as possible followed by axial and scheme coding as shown in Figures 2.1–2.4.

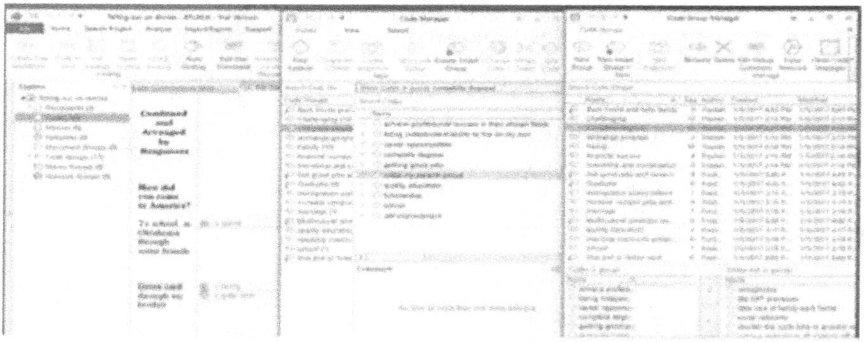

Figure 2.1 Data coding stage one

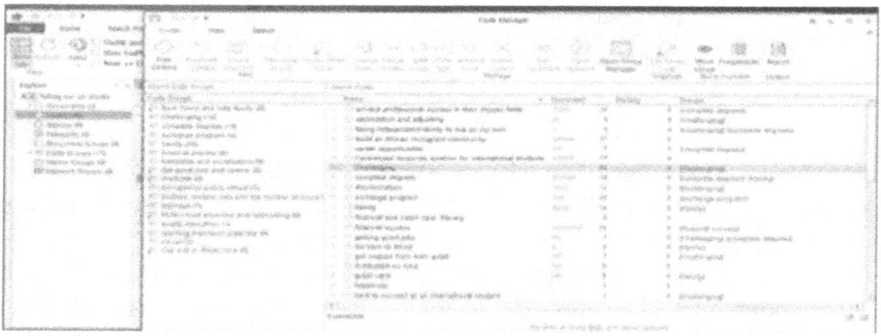

Figure 2.2 The initial 49 codes selected

Figure 2.3 Whole document word cloud

Another challenge included the process where researchers observed the frequencies and intensity of occurrences of a concept as displayed by the software and making memos and code notes. The process enabled the researcher to identify patterns in the data and to search data to help answer

Figure 2.4 Whole document sample of wordlist frequency

the research questions. Despite the challenges, using software not only made the process faster and neater but it also enhanced the reliability, credibility of interpretations, and validity/trustworthiness of findings by producing analysis, creating, inserting, and indexing codes and constructing hyperlinks that made it easy to retrieve selected segments within the text. It also made it convenient to store and display large amounts of qualitative data without becoming concerned about space or how to view multiple segments at once as shown in Figures 2.1–2.3.

Please note that the images presented here are not necessarily for visual value, but are used to demonstrate our process.

Word crunch, although alphabetical, was another challenge as it was too huge a list to be significantly useful to the project (see Figure 2.4). Word cloud (Figure 2.3) was preferred because it sieved the frequently used words. More than three levels of coding were used to ensure the rigor of data analysis thereafter, constituting yet another challenge. The first open coding level was done concurrently with rereading and listening deeply to the content to identify constructs as outlined in the theoretical and conceptual section. The second level was a bit structural and was linked to the research questions. The third level was to start the process of identifying recurrent patterns from the intensity observed from the frequencies (Figures 2.1–2.4). The next two levels were focused on narrowing down the patterns and combining them into themes.

From the responses and guided by the research questions, the researchers focused on the emerging groups of concepts, similar and different major experiences, and participants' opinions and values within the context of being international students and African-born immigrants in the United States. These were what were indexed and used as codes. Coded data as shown in Figures 2.1–2.4 was then filtered, recoded, and further color coded to narrow down the frequent codes, which were then screened for the most recurrent and eventually into themes and subthemes.

Five major themes that seemed to answer the research questions and support literature review section that were revealed from the data included the challenges of being an immigrant in the United States, perception and definition of success, racism and discrimination, coping strategies, and the myth of completing degrees and going back home (Table 2.8). Subthemes included how they came to the United States, their experiences, comparing their success to others who came before them, and the Optional Practical Training (OPT) process.

Data Analysis

The categories from the coding process were then further sorted into recurring themes. All narratives related to a particular theme were placed under that theme. For example, those categories that highlighted the challenges of being an immigrant were grouped together, just as were those on success, racism, coping, and myth of going back home.

Table 2.8 Themes, subthemes, and frequency of responses (percent)

Research question phrase	Theme	Subtheme
How did you come to America? Why did you come to America? How has your experience as a continental African immigrant in America been like?	Challenges of being an immigrant in the United States	How they came to the United States
What does success mean to you?	Perception and definition of success	Failure is not an option
What are the personal expectations/goals you set when you arrived in America? What are the expectations/goals that your family set for you/expected of you?	The myth of completing degrees and going back home	Coping strategies
If you were to make a suggestion to your State Representative about resources and support that immigrants would like to see happen, what would that be?	Their recommendations on further support for international students	Coaching and mentoring

Figure 2.5 Coming to America

The majority of the participants cited school as the main reason why they came or were sponsored to the United States. Others came with the hope of getting jobs and making money so as to live a good life as well as support their families back home while others came to join family and/or their spouses. The major visa categories were student and green card. The statements below summarize respondents' reasons for coming to America:

The exchange program that was aligned with the local university.
I came to totally do personal improvement. I realized it was only America that could sustain my faith to improve myself.
School brought me to America.
I came to visit, then I got married and started a family and I just stayed, later on I went to school.
I won the Diversity Visa lottery.

Figure 2.6 Major reason: school to complete degrees

Figure 2.7 Life and school in the United States is challenging

Figure 2.8 Challenges to achieving success

The main reason for coming to the United States was school with the goal of getting their degrees and either going back home or using those degrees to get good jobs in the United States or back home. Unfortunately, some of them did not have their dreams come true for a variety of reasons, including finances, cultural challenges, illness, or the opportunity to work and thus getting distracted from studies.

Most participants said, "Life on your own in the US is hard. Those who come after us should have an easier life here in the US if they knew from us what we have experienced." The reasons they gave for life as an international student being hard and challenging included:

As a foreigner, being ridiculed, stereotyped.
Language barrier was very humiliating.
International students are burdened with so many credit hours per semester even if they are not working it is too much knowing what other factors they are struggling with.
Option to work more hours, and a revision of the restrictions of working off campus.
I lived in a predominantly White state and even in church where you are expecting to be better accepted they move away from you and sit on another bench and you can see you are not accepted. In school it was hard to get a friend or a project partner because of my accent.

Most of the participants who were students were still struggling academically with full-time classes and full-time low-wage jobs on campus. Although some managed to get their degrees, it was hard to get jobs outside campus or OPT. Others were still struggling to get scholarships and/or teaching assistantships to pay for school. Major challenges cited that hindered their success included:

In terms of academic success and achieving a bachelor's degree, it was both my parents' and my expectation.
My family's expectations for me were to graduate, get a job, and send them money, because I am the most educated and so the expectations to support them financially is higher.
The exchange program did not have enough support and the orientation program was very brief and so much information all in a week and then after that you are on your own and no follow up.
My experience socially we feel very isolated, from African Americans you don't feel like you have much in common with them.

The expectation that once done with school they would go back home and contribute to national success and development has become a mirage for many. For most, their dreams have not been realized, and they are either accepting the situation and settling, or getting disillusioned. At first, their dreams were clear and the future was bright and hopeful as indicated by some of their statements.

... go back home yet I don't have enough savings, so I am thinking about that. But I would like in future to invest in US and my home country.

After completing education and struggling to get jobs and/or OPT, they become disillusioned:

> They expected me to be done with my education and go back home to work in a big company and earn a lot of money.
> Well, my parents wanted me to finish school and come back home and work there.
> My life here has been very unsuccessful. I came here with intention of finishing my degree but got a lot of setbacks and I gave up on school and decided to work on meager jobs to support my family.
> Some get married to Americans to get papers and to get jobs, so they can support themselves and their families back home.

Researchers' Bias and the Phenomenologist's Challenge: Researchers' Reflection and Immersion in the Research

When we were envisioning this research, we did not realize just how challenging it was going to be in terms of bracketing and being objective as expected of phenomenological studies. Being the observer, whose background and experiences are so similar to the observed/the interviewees, posed a challenge of introducing bias into the study. Although we made every effort to control such bias, we are here sharing our stories from our lived experiences, for the sake of clarifying and also presenting the challenges. Both researchers are immigrants from sub-Saharan Africa, but from different regions. One is from the East and the other from the West of Africa.

What was interesting and challenging at the same time was how the major issues and themes raised in this study mirror the lived experiences of both the researchers themselves and those of the interviewees.

The major themes that the researchers wove into their reflection include the challenges of being an immigrant in the United States, perception and definition of success, racism and discrimination, coping strategies, and the myth of completing degrees and going back home. Subthemes include how they came to the United States, their experiences, comparing their success to others who came before them, and where they are now.

Researchers' Reflection: Mariam Konaté, PhD

I am originally from a small French-speaking landlocked country in the heart of West Africa, right in the North of Ghana, called Burkina Faso. Both of my parents were born and raised in Mali, and so was I. I was born in a small town in the North of Mali, in the heart of the Sahara Desert, between the borders of Libya and Algeria, called Tessalit. I am the second oldest of six children.

I had studied English as my major in college. After I graduated from college in Burkina Faso, I did a master's degree in Anglophone African literature as my focus. There was no PhD program in my area of specialization. So, when the opportunity to study in the United States presented itself to me, I did not hesitate to seize it.

My father was the only provider, and as such I have always felt morally obligated to support my parents financially. From the moment I was a college student back home, I had started contributing to household expenses. When I was in college in Burkina Faso, I had a state-sponsored scholarship that provided me with a monthly stipend. When I came to the United States, I continued to supplement my income, despite the fact that I was an international student who was not authorized to work full-time because of my immigration status, and I was living off a meager stipend.

As a sub-Saharan African woman who migrated to the United States, I felt that my parents' expectations of me shifted significantly the moment I arrived in the United States. The understanding that many people from my country, including my own parents, had in the 1990s about the United States, and still have until this day, is that the United States is a country where anyone can make money effortlessly. I came to learn later on from my mother that people were saying that they did not understand why I had not yet built a big house for my parents, notwithstanding the fact that my father already had his own house and thus did not need me to build him another. They were also wondering why I was not sending my parents a lot more money, since I was living in the United States. In the minds of many family and friends, I was a success story because I went to the United States to further my education and increase my chance of a better financial life. Many associated going abroad with financial success and were thus expecting to see me show off that success by lavishing my parents with expensive material things.

As a transnational citizen, I lived simultaneously in two diametrically opposite worlds. Indeed, although I was physically living in the United States, I was at the same time living my life according to my West African cultural and social norms. I was in touch with my parents and family, took care of their financial needs, as well as contributed emotionally and socially to their day-to-day life. I kept in touch with my close high school and college friends. Many times, I was called upon to solve issues that my parents were having with my siblings and/or other family members. I also had to play the role of counselor because all of a sudden my opinion mattered more now that I was living in the United States. I gained some type of "power" linked to my physical presence in America. I came to understand the meaning of that "power" when I first went back home to visit. All of a sudden, people were treating me as if I were no longer one of them, as if I were an "American" with lots of money and "power." They were expecting to notice significant changes in the way that I related to them, as well as in the way that I behaved in general, to fit the idea that they had created in their minds about me. They thought I would start acting as if I were better than anyone else and as an "American." They were thus shocked to realize that I was still pretty much the same down-to-earth person. My own siblings were surprised to notice that I would ask for some of the foods that we grew up eating. They were expecting me to be more picky about what I eat, and were thus pleasantly surprised to realize that I had not begun to look down on important aspects of my cultural identity.

Such is, I believe, the dilemma that most of us African immigrants find ourselves in, as we tread a fine line between two worlds and sets of values. That is what it means to be a transnational citizen, and it is certainly not an easy balance to maintain, as we have to constantly juggle to find a healthy middle ground between the two cultures. For example, although I was living thousands of miles away on a different continent, I was and still am very much a part of their lives, as well as I was a constant presence in theirs. I was expected to solve financial emergencies. Whenever I felt that I had saved enough money for my emergency fund, something would happen back home, and I would be called upon to solve that financial issue. I felt like I could never breathe long enough.

What I learned from my experience as a sub-Saharan African immigrant is that it is very important to remain anchored in my culture because my cultural values have provided me with the foundation and direction that I needed to surmount many challenges in this country. No matter how long I have lived in this country, I will never culturally be an "American." As a proverb in Bambanankan goes, "No matter how long a tree trunk has remained under water, it will never turn into a crocodile." My identity as an African woman living in the American context has allowed me to take a critical look at some of the patriarchal practices of my culture and question them, especially those that are sexist and detrimental to the ideals of fairness and aim at subjugating women.

A second lesson that I have learned is to stick to one's plans and goals and to be focused on achieving them because one can be easily derailed from one's initial goals once they get to America.

A third lesson would be to speak up and to advocate for oneself, whether in one's relationship, or socially in general. The weight of patriarchy and racism can easily make someone feel inadequate, less than, and powerless. Thus, having a voice and expressing how one feels could prevent one from feeling victimized, oppressed, silenced, or devalued. We should feel neither ashamed nor embarrassed to share our stories with other immigrants because we might realize that we are experiencing the same situation, a realization that can help us feel less isolated and alone.

And finally, seeking a support system, asking for help when we need it is very important for keeping our sanity. The moral support and understanding from people who are experiencing similar situations cannot be stressed enough.

Researchers' Reflection: Fredah Mainah, PhD

I am originally from a former British colony in East Africa called Kenya. I was born in a village that is about an hour away from Nairobi, the capital city of Kenya. Because of its proximity to the capital, I was a child of two worlds: when school was in session, my family lived on a small farm that our father had bought near his ancestral village, while during school holidays we lived in the city with our father at an apartment provided by his employer.

The main languages spoken are English, inherited from the colonizer, and Kiswahili, a local Bantu language. Today the country is famous for its tourist destinations that attract millions of tourists from all over the world for its beautiful equatorial weather and its wildlife. It is also one of the fastest growing economies in Africa after South Africa and Nigeria.

Growing up in two worlds like that gave me opportunities that most of my village- and classmates did not have. I grew up connected to our ancestral home and its culture as well as exposed to foreign cultures and languages, both locally and internationally. Locally, living in a cosmopolitan environment during school holidays, I interacted with people from other local communities/tribes from across the country.

More education opened my eyes to other economic opportunities, and in 2005, I left Kenya and went to Botswana, another African country near South Africa. In Botswana, I worked as an education consultant as well as a performance and productivity researcher and instructor. While living and working in Botswana, my daughter revisited her own career dream and asked me to support her to go to the United States for further studies. At the time I was not earning enough to support her. However, another opportunity presented itself for her. She got a volunteer position with an international nonprofit organization and was posted to Nigeria, a country to the west in Africa. While there, an American decided to sponsor her visa application, accommodation in the United States, and tuition for a whole year!

With my daughter in the United States, it was an easy decision to make to immigrate to join her. In 2008, my son and I embarked on the immigrant journey to America. Today I am a college professor teaching diversity and leadership and other African American and African studies courses.

I had come to the United States through a Diversity Visa lottery called the Green Card. Everyone assumes that this is a pass to all American privileges. When I first got to the United States, I thought, armed with a Green Card and with all my education and experience, it would be easy to get a job or start my own consultancy. I soon discovered that credentials from Africa were not easily recognized here and quickly went back to school and got another master's degree and later a PhD, regardless of the student debt that came with it.

As much as I would like to be the best educator, author, activist for the rights of all beings, and an engaged scholar committed to my community, I never feel like I belong. In some instances, I am the only Black person in a space and at other times, although with other Black people, I am still an outsider from my homeland of Africa.

References

Chothia, Farouk. 2013. "How Welcome Are Africans in the UK?" BBC World. www.bbc.com/news/world-africa-25111177.

Colaizzi, Paul F. 1978. "Psychological Research as the Phenomenologist Views It." In *Existential Phenomenological Alternatives for Psychology*, edited by Ronald S. Valle and Mark King, 48–71. New York: Oxford University Press.

Creswell, John W. 2014. *Research Design: Qualitative, Quantitative and Mixed Methods Approaches*. Los Angeles: Sage.

Denzin, N. 1989. *Interpretive Biography*. London: Sage.

Denzin, Norman K. and Yvonna S. Lincoln. 1994. *Handbook of Qualitative Research*. Thousand Oaks, CA: Sage.

Fisher, Linda and Lester Embree, eds. 2000. *Feminist Phenomenology*. Dordrecht: Kluwer.

Giorgi, Amedeo. 2009. *The Descriptive Phenomenological Method in Psychology: A Modified Husserlian Approach*. Pittsburgh, PA: Duquesne University Press.

Green, Chris. 2015. "Immigration Policy Led to 'New Forms of Racism,' Says New Study." *The Independent*. March 1, 2015. www.independent.co.uk/news/uk/home-news/immigration-policy-led-to-new forms-of-racism-says-new-study-10078876.html.

Hein, Serge F. and Wendy J. Austin. 2001. "Empirical and Hermeneutic Approaches to Phenomenological Research in Psychology: A Comparison." *Psychological Methods* 6: 3–17. Doi:10.1037/1082–989X.6.1.3.

hooks, bell. 1989. *Talking Back: Thinking Feminist, Thinking Black*. Vol. 10. New York: South End Press.

Kent, Mary. 2007. "Immigration and America's Black Population." *Population Bulletin*. 62, no. 4: 1–135.

Knox, S. and Burkard, A.W. 2009. Qualitative Research Interviews. Psychotherapy Research.

Moustakas, C. 1994. *Phenomenological Research Methods*. Thousand Oaks, CA: Sage.

Pew Research Center. 2013. *African Immigrant Population in U.S. Steadily Climbs.* Retrieved from https://www.google.com/search?q=Pew+Research+Center.+(2013)&oq=Pew+Resear ch+Center.+(2013)&aqs=chrome..69i57j0l5.2799j0j8&sourceid=chrome&es_sm=93 &ie=UTF-8#q=black+immigrant+population%2C+Pew+Research+Center+(2013).

Redway, Jorja. 2014. "Black Caribbean Immigrants in the United States and Their Perceptions of Racial Discrimination: Understanding the Impact of Racial Identity, Ethnic Identity and Racial Socialization." PhD dissertation, Columbia University. http:dx.doi.org/10.7916/D8VT1Q8Q.

Roulston, Kathryn. 2010. *Reflective Interviewing: A Guide to Theory and Practice.* London: Sage.

Saldana, J. 2011. *Fundamentals of Qualitative Research.* New York: Oxford University Press.

Seidman, I. E. 1991. *Interviewing as Qualitative Research.* New York: Teachers College Press.

Simms, E.M. and Stawarska, B. 2013. Introduction: Concepts and Methods in Interdisciplinary Feminist Phenomenology. *Janus Head* 13, no. 1: 6–16.

Somerville, Will, Dhananjayan Sriskandarajah, and Maria Latorre. 2009. "United Kingdom: A Reluctant Country of Immigration." *Migration Information Source.* July 21, 2009. Migration Policy Institute. www.migrationpolicy.org/article/united-kingdom-reluctant-country-immigration.

US Census Bureau Report 2019. "Foreign Born." www.census.gov/topics/population/foreign-born.html.

Appendix 1: Interview Protocol

Participants will be asked the following questions. The interview will take 45 minutes and will be recorded using a digital recorder. Researchers will review the informed consent document before starting the interview, and they will remind participants of the voluntary nature of this research study. Researchers may also answer any questions participants might have. Researchers will refer to participants by number so that they can protect the identity of the participant.

Bio Form

1. What is your age?
2. What is your gender?
3. What is the highest degree you have achieved?
4. How long have you been in the United Stated?

Interview Questions

1. How did you come to America?
2. Why did you come to America?
3. How has your experience as a continental African immigrant in America been like?
4. What are the personal expectations/goals you set when you arrived in America?

5. What are the expectations/goals that your family set for you/expected of you?

6. What does success mean to you?

7. Has your nationality and/or gender hindered or helped you in any way?

   If so, how?
   If not, how do you explain that?

8. Do you know people from your country and/or other African countries who have come here and have been successful?

9. What does their success look like? Describe their success.

10. Do you know people from other African countries who have come here and who have not been successful? What does that look like?

11. Has living in a different culture with different values impacted your marriages? If so, how and why?

12. If you were to make a suggestion to your state representative about resources and support that immigrants would like to see happen, what would that be?

13. How is being an immigrant in the West? (United States, Canada, UK, Australia)

Thank you for sharing your story with us.

Chapter 3

BEING A SUB-SAHARAN AFRICAN
IMMIGRANT IN THE UNITED STATES:
SPEAKING FROM THE HEART IN
A FOREIGN LANGUAGE

*After the Egyptian and Indian, the Greek and Roman, the Teuton and Mongolian,
the Negro is a sort of seventh son, born with a veil, and gifted with second sight
in this American world, a world, which yields him no true self-consciousness, but only
lets him see himself through the revelation of the other world. It is a peculiar sensation,
this double-consciousness, this sense of always looking at one's self through the eyes of
others, of measuring one's soul by the tape of a world that looks on in amused contempt
and pity. One ever feels his twoness, an American, a Negro; two souls, two thoughts,
two unreconciled strivings; two warring ideals in one dark body, whose dogged strength
alone keeps it from being torn asunder.*

—W. E. B. Du Bois, *The Souls of Black Folk*

Among the many challenges sub-Saharan African immigrants face is the issue of being viewed as different yet expected to assimilate and behave as an American. To delve deeper into the identity crises that many African immigrants are experiencing, the authors use this chapter to discuss the issues related to the inner struggles that sub-Saharan African immigrants experience as they navigate between two worlds. The authors also explore how their resilience wanes and how their values and expectations evolve and change over time as a result of the pressures to adjust and assimilate. This chapter also explores the issues of trying to assimilate and fit in the American culture, negotiating race, class and gender biases, and other plurilingual challenges.

We start with language as a dimension for identification that is used more often due to the difference in accent when African immigrants speak in the United States. Then we progress to the definition of selfhood as a navigational tool towards assimilation and immersion into the United States culture. In this chapter, we also explore communication as a general tool for adaptation, assimilation, education and economic pursuits, productivity and being in a world where a slight detection of a different accent other than American English can cause one to be not only viewed, but also evaluated as being incompetent.

Research indicates that there is a relationship between identity and a sense of belonging, motivation, achievement, persistence, eventual success and general well-being. According to the communication theory of identity created by Michael Hecht, Jennifer Warren, Eura Jung and Janice Krieger (2005), our identities are informed by both a naturally communicative and a relational influence. Hecht et al. go on to state that our identities are situated in and influenced by four interrelated frames. The first one is the "personal frame," which consists of how we self-identify. The second one is the "enacted frame," which refers to how we communicate our identity to others. The third one is the "relational frame," and it involves aspects of our identity that are expressed when we interact with others. Finally, the last frame is the "communal frame," which describes how our identity is shaped by communities with which we interact.

Cheikh Anta Diop's (1981) theory of cultural identity argues that there is a continuous shared culture among African people formed around cultural identity and based on three factors: (1) a historical factor (colonization and the issue of Egypt being classified as a European country among other factors); (2) a linguistic factor (the annihilation of African languages and being replaced with European languages as one among many factors affecting indigenous languages and peoples); and (3) a psychological factor (mental well-being, caused by the effects of colonization and dehumanizing of Africans, a biased historical record that categorizes Africans as subhumans).

Fares Karam (2018), in research on language and identity, argues that language, in its multimodal and multilingual dimensions, is a key resource for identification and selfhood, and as such immigrants from non-English-speaking countries need to learn not only how to speak it but also how to use it to express and demonstrate identity and agency in a foreign country. Those who emigrate from English-speaking countries have to contend with always being excluded, isolated, and at best, being asked to repeat what they said in a conversation or meeting because of their foreign English accents. Years of learning and practice in a foreign language are discounted and invalidated by that slight moment of listening and judging an accent as unacceptable and the speaker as incompetent and unworthy of listening to.

This discounting, devaluing, and invalidating has a historical basis. The trade in enslaved Africans that started in the sixteenth century has depleted the African continent of its most valuable resources: people. As the Transatlantic Slave Trade was officially abolished in 1808, a new era of the balkanization of the entire continent was about to begin. Indeed, the Berlin Conference of 1884–1885 divided up the African continent among European imperialist countries. By the beginning of the twentieth century, the entire African continent, except Liberia and Ethiopia, had been divided up like a cake between European colonial powers, each wanting to get the biggest slice.

The scramble for Africa ushered in the colonial occupation and exploitation of African countries. With the new colonial order came the imposition of Western power and cultures, and especially language, on newly colonized African nations. As a result, African nations lost their autonomy and sovereignty. They also lost their cultures, languages, educational systems, and religions. European colonial powers sought to colonize Africans politically, economically, religiously, and culturally. To that end, they imposed Christianity along with a colonial educational system that was designed to mentally and culturally alienate Africans and brainwash the colonized Africans to look down on their own cultures, languages, and customs. As part of the civilizing mission, colonized Africans were no longer allowed to speak their indigenous languages in schools and in designated official administrative spaces. Instead, they were forced to speak the language of their colonizers. The cultural alienation that resulted from the imposition of the colonial mentality has led to an identity crisis among many colonized Africans, the manifestations of which are still noticeable today. Among them are the abandonment of African cultures, languages, the aping of Western ways, and the practice of depigmentation in order to become White Black people. Yet this whole history, the reason for their accent, or their seeming timidity is ignored when listening to a sub-Saharan African immigrant in the United States.

As we interviewed our 25 respondents, these issues kept coming up. Some of them dismissed them, while others were confused by how such a trivial matter as accent was taking center stage in a discussion about a job offer, or a class discussion about global issues or just a coffee conversation that took a turn away from the bonding exercise it was meant to be.

Introducing the theory of intermediality to discuss the idea of African identity based on Blackness, accent, and resulting issues of exclusion and discrimination, Kalua (2020) argues that such a notion is flawed because African identity is not fixed on one dimension of Blackness. Intermediality in this context is used in relation to the immigrant's ability to be both the medium of communication and the participant in the communication, as in the use of multiple discourses and sensory modalities of interaction simultaneously. An immigrant learner, for example, may be code switching when communicating at home or in their mind while in the classroom learning and doing a media project, and reflecting on the whole process in a different language than the language of instruction. This in itself presents the challenge of how to define such a learner just as Black and not one who is multiskilled at expressing themselves, communicating, as well as participating in multiple discourses and in multiple languages and cultures.

Derwing and Munro (2009) argue that as a salient aspect of speech, speaking with an accent that is viewed as other or different, and worse still from a foreign country, has negative social, psychological, and communicative consequences because of the unrealistic expectation that all speakers use a similar accent that is correlated with the dominant people and culture. They further argue that because of their foreign accents and the fear of being stereotyped, immigrants may experience further anxiety and pressure to redefine their identity in order to avoid other negative stereotypes and threats emanating from workplaces, communities where they live, as well as institutions of education. Imitating local accents is a typical way of coping and assimilating into such environments.

On the issue of assimilation, adaptation, and integration, Waters and Jiménez (2005) use four benchmarks of assimilation, including socioeconomic status, spatial concentration, language assimilation, and intermarriage in their attempt to come up with theories about immigrant assimilation. They argue that such theories will be beneficial in the planning for assimilation activities and for assessing integration and assimilation programs.

Speaking on the issue of immigrants who arrive in their host countries already speaking multiple languages, Patricia Halagao (2017) urges educators and policymakers to make an effort to meet their multilingual needs by availing resources, equalizing organizational support and staff, and valuing plurilingual skills, given that most schools are increasingly becoming more ethnically diverse. Craythorne (2006) focuses on how identity is influenced by the strategies of adaptation and assimilation amidst racism in the United States, while Schotte et al. (2017) focus on the issue of integration and whether that assists in adaptation, cultural identity, and academic achievement.

Our respondents not only had lived experiences to share about their adaptation and assimilation, they also had suggestions and recommendations on how to assist in this process. For example, they suggested meeting with representatives of the local area where they live to explore ways in which this could be programmed. They also thought that higher education could increase involvement in the local communities and set up language centers where immigrants could be assisted in learning American English.

The literature reviewed and discussed in this chapter (Crofty 1998; Waters and Jiménez 2005; Craythorne 2006; Council of Europe 2001, 2007; Derwing and Munro 2009; Halagao 2017; Schotte et al. 2017; Karam 2018; Johnson 2019; Kalua 2020) shows that immersion and assimilation of current immigrants into the American society and its dominant culture, and of particular interest, into the educational system, is driven by dimensions such as socioeconomic status, language assimilation, accent and appropriate pronunciation, intelligibility, negative stereotypes, conformance fatigue, intermarriage, sharing, inclusion and acceptance, sociocultural competence, political integration, and spatial concentration. Johnson (2019) argues that racial hierarchies largely influence the shaping of identities and integration of Black immigrants, while Crofty (1998) argues for individualized and contextual meaning making to negotiate identity and its redefinition and reconstruction.

The Council of Europe (2001) recognizes translanguaging and plurilingualism as a characteristic of individuals, as opposed to multilingualism that is a societal characteristic. From that perspective, it defines plurilingualism as the ability of a student and/or citizen to demonstrate proficiency in the use of other learned languages and cultures to communicate and to take part in intercultural action. In its endeavor to ensure political and economic cohesion, the Council advocates for the support and increased access to language practices, identities, and ways of knowing, as well as learning, in an inclusive environment. The Council's emphasis was on acknowledging, recognizing, and supporting the value of citizens who have other language and intercultural competencies gained from the lived experiences of being immersed in other multiple cultures besides the named language of the host country as a way to support and ease the burden of learners coming into monolingual school systems.

The notion of plurilingualism was adopted by the Council of Europe (2001) as an approach toward language education policy in Europe and has since been used more widely in applied linguistics research as a way to more equitably view diverse communicative resource use. As per the Council's guidelines (2007), plurilingualism is the ability of a person who has competence in more than one language to switch between multiple languages depending on the situation for ease of communication. Plurilinguals practice multiple languages and can switch between them when necessary, without too much difficulty. Although plurilingualism is derived from multilingualism (also referred to as bilingualism), there is a difference between the two. Multilingualism is connected to situations wherein multiple languages exist side by side in a society but are utilized separately. In essence, multilingualism is the coexisting knowledge of separate languages, while plurilingualism is the interconnected knowledge of multiple languages. In general, Plurilinguals have had contact with languages not native to them through educational institutions, however, the education system plays only a small role in the linguistic competence of these individuals.

Learning a second language is thought to stimulate someone's plurilingualism. Immigrants who emigrate already speaking multiple languages cannot always be described as bilingual or multilingual because speaking and communicating in more than one named language in a monolingual environment has its own unique historical and sociopolitical challenges embedded in that environment. When plurilinguals immigrate to a country that speaks a language not in their repertoire, they are burdened with the task of having to learn yet another language, as well as another culture. If they are students, that increases their academic burden. It also increases the pressure of assimilation and all other problems that come as a result of the need to adapt and settle in a new environment and culture.

When they do learn the host language, it is treated as a language requirement and not as a second language or a sociocultural competence as happens when a monolingual learns another language. García and Otheguy (2019), while making a case for plurilingualism and translanguaging, argue that in a monolingual environment, power differentials created through colonialism and imperialism favor the monolinguals that learn another language at school, considering it a challenge that requires extra resources and support while at the same time discounting the same challenges when experienced by those who already speak multiple languages. This is especially so for immigrants from former colonial countries who had their own native languages and have now adopted their colonial masters' languages as official and as languages of instruction, while retaining their own native languages for communication at home.

Throughout this chapter, plurilingual and pluricultural will be treated as competences since they demonstrate an ability "to use languages for the purposes of communication and to take part in intercultural action, where a person, viewed as a social agent, has proficiency, of varying degrees, in several languages and experience of several cultures" (Council of Europe 2007, 10). Further, the use will include the recognition of mother tongues of the immigrants as named languages. The authors' argument is based on the consideration of what constitutes a foreign language in the twenty-first century bearing in mind how reductive such a definition is to many African languages that are demeaned by colonial legacy.

The Council of Europe (2007, 10) clarifies issues of note as it relates to description of multilingualism and bilingualism: "This area of intervention will be called language education policies (in order to stress that it is not only a question of dealing with the subject in technical terms, as in the field of educational 'engineering' and language teaching methods), whether they concern national or 'foreign' languages, those known as mother tongues, or second languages, majority or minority languages, and so on. On the contrary, this document emphasizes the central place of languages of every kind and education systems in the social problems that have to be confronted in Europe on the basis of common principles."

Linking literacy and competence to orality in English (or any other colonial language), and eventually to cognition, intellectual capacity, and capability, privileges the native language speaker while disadvantaging and excluding the plurilinguals. Literacy is a social practice and standardization is an impediment to learning and teaching that provides skills and knowledge to mediate the self in relation to one's identity, and social and cultural context.

How literacy is defined and reported is biased and skewed towards Eurocentric, languages and criteria of literacy. Those literacy data never include literacy in indigenous African languages even though many Africans are literate in those and not in European languages. For example, using just a few of the countries: Equatorial New Guinea has a population of 1,402,983 and a literacy rate of 95.3 percent; South Africa, despite apartheid policies, has a population of 59,308,690 and a literacy rate of 94.3 percent; Libya's population is 6,871,292 and literacy rate is 91 percent; Mauritius has a population of 1,271,768 and a literacy rate of 90.6 percent; Botswana has a population of 2,351,627 and a literacy rate of 88.5 percent; Zimbabwe has a population of 14,862,924 and despite its economic and political turmoil that lasted for many decades, it has a literacy rate of 86.5 percent; Rwanda, despite a genocide that saw over 800,000 of its population dead in a 100 days, now has a population of 11,890,784 and a literacy rate of 85.6 percent; Kenya, today referred to as an economic giant of East Africa, has a population of 52.6 million people and a literacy rate of 81.5 percent; Burkina Faso has a population of 16 million and a literacy rate of 41.2 percent; Mali has a population of 21 million and a literacy of 35.4 percent; Gabon has a population of 2,225,734 and a literacy rate of 83.2 percent; Nigeria has a population of 212 million and a literacy rate of 62 percent; and Ethiopia has a population of 115 million and a literacy rate of 52 percent.

Immigrants are not only code breakers, who must decode systems of written and spoken languages, visual images, local myths, heroes and their stories, and other nuances, but can also be supported to move beyond rote memorization of words and phrases to become meaning makers in the newly learned and adopted language and culture. How many opportunities have minorities in our universities missed or been excluded from because of how language and linguistics are used to exclude these communities from social, political, and economic opportunities by authorizing, legitimating, naturalizing, and opening paths only to those who speak what is constructed as the common, autonomous and whole national language.

This state of things reflects the lived experiences of some of our respondents who said the following:

> My nationality has helped me in a sense that I can speak more than one language and I have been able to educate a lot of people about our way of life. It has also hindered me especially in job opportunities. Americans are usually more preferred than us who are foreigners even though I am a permanent resident.
>
> [...] Coming to America from an Anglophone speaking African country I don't have much problem in terms of integration particularly in terms of being able to speak and communicate in English but there are Africans or other immigrants who come from non-English-speaking countries, that is, French, Portuguese, or Spanish speaking countries. What I have found is that several African colleagues have brought wives from non-English-speaking countries and for years their wives are not able to work because they don't have the command of the English language, so I think. [...] I know that there are organizations that help immigrants to integrate but I should think that language education from non-English speakers should be given and should continue to be supported with resources to enable those immigrants who want to integrate to be able to learn the English language and be proficient in the language so they can be gainfully employed and productive members of society.

From such responses, there is a clear indication that respondents felt a need to deal with the issues of redefining their identity, some personal and group beliefs, norms, and values, and an even further need to expand their worldview. Their skin color, for example, had suddenly become a dimension of their identity, and they did not know how to deal with that. Having learned and used English all their school life, they could not understand how their accent was a communication issue. This perspective of translanguaging rests on the idea that the concept of the named language and the related concepts of language purity and verbal hygiene were constructed to support ideologies of racial, class, and gender superiority.

Other respondents struggled with these and similar issues and had the following to say:

> Yes, being Black in American society like I have explained earlier on does have its own disadvantages. You will experience racial discrimination in one form or the other. But having lived in Canada for four years before coming to the United States I already know what the racial situation is and so one is very prepared to face any form of discrimination.

In this book and from a constructivist approach, the authors argue that identity need not be fixed or based on some culturally constructed bias. If identity is relational and discoursally constructed, and as such constantly changing and not fixed, then it is necessary that it be redefined, and it ought to reflect an individual's desire to identify with a social practice that they want to establish or a sense of belonging to a self-selected group, as is the case of sub-Saharan immigrants.

In his research on African-Caribbean immigrants in the United States, Johnson (2019) found similar issues as the authors are discussing here. He stated that African-Caribbean immigrants whom he interviewed described an experience of "sudden realization, or epiphany, about race in America. In addition to becoming aware of the different reality of race in America from the Caribbean, the participants described becoming aware that the American perspective on race subjected them to ill-treatment simply because they are Black" (Johnson 2019, 67).

Our respondents struggled with identity and issues of becoming aware and being confronted by racism, just as Johnson (2019) had found in his research. Using words and phrases such as "it dawned on me," "I realized," and so on, our respondents described their experience of being treated differently and having to reassess and reconstruct their identity. One respondent shared that:

It has had its phases, when I first came, I was very excited but then it quickly dawned on me that I was different which I kind of liked because it gave me friends who were curious of my heritage. That curiosity soon wore off and I began trying to assimilate, disassociating myself from everything African. I ended up being apart of an accelerated program for high schoolers and by my junior year I was the only Black person in my class. I realized all the non-immigrant and American people at the school didn't consider me African or Black because "I was Black but not Black Black" (sic. African American). That angered me and in my junior year I began to love everything about my ethnicity, I celebrated the fact that I was an immigrant, that I was educated, and I had dreams and goals. My pride as an African, my literacy in African history grew. Now I demand respect for my differences.

From this comment, we can see that this respondent has gone through the phases of arriving, facing dissonance, and incongruence; struggled with discrimination; and eventually has assertively decided that they will navigate, assimilate, and redefine themselves in their own terms.

Other respondents had the following to say about their experiences:

You know what? It has been challenging, I think the key challenge is balancing our culture and trying to adapt and assimilate within the American culture and yet still hold onto our own. That is the part that is very challenging.

Not as a student but once I got to work it was hard not to notice that I was getting paid less because of gender and race.

Yes, for nationality. Working in a predominantly White company my accent is made fun of, then I stand out since I am the only one in my department, my view point is sometimes ignored, then stereotypes that I have to debunk and being everyone's teacher about Africa and African students.

When compelled to use English language as the only way to demonstrate one's talents and innovation, as a measure of competence and success, or as a way to define one's socioeconomic status, the respondents had the following to add:

For the most part it has been positive, there were expected difficulties at the beginning while I was trying to figure out how to navigate living in a new culture/society.

Great and challenging, One has to work harder here and the working days are long. In Africa the expectations are low and we are not as hard working. Working days are shorter and there are no multiple shifts. Working culture and ethics are also different.

I have had to adapt a lot; the first thing was the fast pace of life. It was the first thing to hit me. Adapting to that fast pace of life, while also adapting to a social system that is very individualistic, I was used to a social structure where there is a lot of support and people tend to look out for one another much more. I found that bit of people keeping to themselves I found it very difficult to adjust to, still struggle with it. I have just had to come to terms with it that people are busy, that's way life is here.

I have learned more about the culture, they have a melting pot kind of culture, have a civilized way of doing things compared to where I come from.

Further sharing from respondents in their own words about in-school and out-of-school activities for immersion and assimilation showed that:

Immigrants have a big problem, when you come to a new country either you adapt to a new country, or you won't succeed. If you come to a new country with a mentality of the other country especially if you take for example Burkina Faso and France and the US. So, in order to succeed in that country, you have to change your mentality and thinking like the people of the country.

When I came to the US, I was really prepared and the gentleman who encouraged me to come to the USA gave me a lot of good advice. Before I came here, I went to the US cultural center and learned about the US so I was prepared when I came here.

The responses, ranging from those of professors to students, were similar. Here is a sample:

As a foreigner, being ridiculed, stereotyped, language barrier was very humiliating.

Most international students are blinded by what they see on the TV before we get here.

I have had students drop off my course because they alleged they could not follow the course because of my accent. Yet I came to the US as teenager and went to school here and have lived here for over forty years! Some of my colleagues from Europe have distinct and heavy accents but they get a pass.

From the report by the Council of Europe (2001, 2007), one can infer that it is detrimental to the immigrant (learner or citizen) when their competence or civic engagement is measured in terms of speech, as it undermines even the scholarly and proficient. If speaking with an accent that is not "acceptable" means that one is not competent in the context of whatever is being handled whether in class or a boardroom, then what line and where should it be drawn as to whose accent is acceptable or not?

Measuring language competence by accent rather than all the years of learning and practice that are devoted to communicating in a foreign language, as well as the language and culture ability and competence, is not only unfair, it is also a disservice to any immigrant. Immigrants spend a lot of school years learning a foreign language and yet get dismissed within a split second of someone listening to them and judging their competence based on their accent. All linguistic, grammar, literary, discourse, and sociolinguistic and sociocultural skills and competencies that they have worked so hard at are dismissed because of the fact that they speak a slightly different variation of English.

For instance, pronunciation and tonal variables in the United States are used to distinguish those from the North from those of the South (Southern drawl, they call it). Yet that is not used to discriminate or disfavor them. Accents from Australia and Europe are also not used against them at least as far as research goes. Why then is it such a big issue for those considered Black? It is no wonder then that sub-Saharan African immigrants link their accents to racism, discrimination, isolation, and exclusion from certain benefits. The effort they make to assimilate and speak in an American accent shows the lengths to which they are willing to go to be accepted.

Using communication theories of maintenance, convergence, and divergence to explore issues of assimilation and adapting, the authors share the following from several study participants who shared their experiences of being the target of linguistic profiling. They reported that the moment they start speaking, they give away the fact that they are not native speakers of English. They reported being constantly told they have a nice accent and being asked where they were from.

However, some reported that their African accent played to their advantage because as continental Africans, they appeared to be less threatening than African Americans. Some of the stereotypes that White Americans use to discriminate and oppress African Americans, at least on an interpersonal level, are not always applied to continental Africans or other African and African diasporic groups.

In the middle of the COVID-19 crisis and the new culture of wearing masks, increased conflicts in and issues with communication might have been faced by sub-Saharan African immigrants. The new communication environment in which we all found ourselves was unique for people who for centuries were used to listening to each other face to face and using facial cues, especially lips, to follow along in a conversation. When facial expressions and mouth gestures are not visible, did the accent issue become even more complex, or were we more compassionate and understanding, perhaps even honing our listening skills? Did the need for someone to smile as they communicated disappear? If so, with what was it replaced? That might make for interesting research.

What is disturbing is that no effort is expected of the listener whose language is the "dominant" one to understand the immigrant with an accent, nor is such effort made by that listener, even while no recognition or appreciation is given for the immigrant speaker who although competent, still has an accent due to L1 (mother tongue) influence. Nonverbal signals, such as a cupped hand to the ear and leaning in to indicate that the listener is not hearing or understanding the immigrant speaker, are also forms of racism and discounting unless in clear cases of hearing disability.

As we conclude, we discuss a coping mechanism that we found common throughout the interviews: silent engagement. It was like a battle between the listening cultures and the speaking cultures.

When attending a multicultural meeting, understanding how different cultures respond to silence can help communication flow. If the majority of the attendees are from a culture where silence is discouraged, they will understand that their colleagues who do not speak up immediately do have something valuable to offer, they merely need some silence before joining the discussion. Conversely, if the majority of the participants are from a country where silence is expected, they will understand that their colleagues who are unusually verbose are not being disrespectful.

When speaking with someone for whom English is not their first language, the person may need time to consider the question, frame an answer, switch codes, and then translate their thoughts into English before responding. If you do not know this, you may inadvertently interrupt the silence and ask the same question in a different way, thinking the person did not understand your first query. Have you ever tried speaking or writing in a language other than your own? It can be a challenge.

Some Western cultures think silence is a sign of lack of engagement in the conversation or even disagreement. Americans, for example, often see silence as indicating the person is indifferent, angry, or disagreeing with them, if not totally incompetent. The silence confuses and confounds them since it is so different from expected behavior. A forced monolingualization process that millions of multilingual immigrants continue to experience compromises their health and well-being. In sociolinguistics, it is common to observe that language learners, when learning to interact in a new language, often experience a period of silent engagement, as demonstrated in the following quotes:

> In 1963, Paul Simon and Art Garfunkel sang about "The Sounds of Silence."
> A West African proverb states, "Silence is also speech."
> In the sixth century, Chinese philosopher Lao Tzu claimed that "Silence is a source of great strength."

Researchers' Reflection: Mariam Konaté, PhD

Growing up, I always moved between different spaces, as my father and my mother were from two totally different ethnic groups. My father's parents were originally from Burkina Faso but immigrated to Mali in the 1930s during the colonial occupation of West Africa by France. My father was born in Mali in 1946. In order to assimilate to their new environment, my grandparents changed their last name from Drabo, which is a common last name in Burkina Faso, to Konaté, which is a common last name in Mali. My father grew up speaking Bambanankan, one of the most commonly spoken languages in Mali, with its variations spoken in many other West African countries.

Both his parents also spoke Samoghokan, their native language from Burkina Faso. My father could understand Samoghokan, but did not speak it fluently.

My mother, on the other hand, is from the Keltamacheq ethnic group. The Keltamacheq are a nomadic ethnic group in the Sahara Desert of the North of Mali, very close to the borders of Libya and Algeria. They are said to be the descendants of the Berber ethnic groups who originated from Yemen.

I was born in the city of Tessalit, Mali, in the Sahara Desert. I speak four indigenous African languages and two European languages (English and French). I took classes in Arabic and German in high school, but I have no skills at all in these ones. The very first language I ever heard and spoke was Keltamacheq, which is my mother tongue. I am still very fluent in speaking it, and I am planning on polishing my writing skills. The second language I spoke was Bambanankan, my father tongue. This one I am proficient in both spoken and written. Because my father was a schoolteacher, he moved a lot for his teaching assignments. Growing up, we would spend two to three years in different parts of Mali, as the government sent my father to his teaching assignments.

Then, when I went to first grade at the age of seven, I had to learn to speak French, which was the third language I ever spoke. Mali was colonized by France. Thus, French is the official language in which education and all official business is conducted. When I was 11 years old, my parents decided to emigrate to Burkina Faso where I had to learn to speak Moore, one of the three commonly spoken languages in Burkina Faso. I was also introduced to Julakan, which is a dialect of Bambanankan. It is a language that was developed as a result of trading among Mali, Burkina Faso, and Ivory Coast. It was much easier for me to speak and write Julakan because I already spoke Bambanakan very fluently. I remember that my father did not want us to speak Julakan because he felt it was a dialectical variation of Bambanankan. I guess he did not want us to lose the "original" language. I remember that he was also very reluctant for any of us, his children, to learn Moore. I never understood my father's position about us learning other languages. I remember that at the very tender age of four and five, my father would not allow me to speak my mother tongue. He would enforce it by physically punishing me for speaking Tamacheq when my maternal grandmother visited or when one of my uncles or anyone on my mother's side of the family who spoke the language visited. Later, when I was in high school and after we had moved to Burkina Faso, he would physically punish me whenever I came back from visiting one of my maternal aunts who spoke Tamacheq.

Then when I was 14 and in seventh grade, I started middle school, and I was introduced to the English language. English is a mandatory subject that all students have to take from 7th through 12th grade. When I was in elementary school in Mali in the mid to late 1970s, teachers had come up with a way to force their students to always speak French, even during recess. To that effect, they came up with a system to make sure that students who did not adhere to the rules were punished. They made a necklace with a wooden donkey carved on it. During school recess, any student caught speaking their African language instead of French was given the donkey necklace to wear. That student was made fun of by everyone during recess, was called a "donkey," laughed at, mocked, and ridiculed by everyone in the school. We were even taught a "donkey song." We were supposed to disparage any student who happened to speak their language instead of French. The song referred to that student as a donkey going to the country of donkeys. That student in turn had to find another student who was speaking their language instead of French and pass the donkey necklace to that student. Any students who went home at the end of the school day with the donkey necklace had to pay a fine to the school the following day.

I remember that the resolve that my father and the schoolteachers had in making me not learn to speak the languages that they felt were "inferior" actually pushed me to learn and excel in them. As a plurilingual person, I sometimes have to think in several languages before speaking in English. I do sometimes experience what linguists refer to as language interference. Because I do have both a strong African and French accent, when I am in meetings or when I do talk to people in general, they tend to think that I am not smart and intelligent or that what I have to say is not important enough. In meetings, it does happen that what I say is not considered important. However, when someone else, usually a White person, says the same thing, it is given immediate attention and appreciation and is affirmed and validated as intelligent and innovative.

In the classroom, students do not seem to make an effort to listen; they create a mental blockage for themselves and allege that they cannot understand the professor just because of a foreign African accent. Foreign European and Australian accents are always considered "cute." Why is it that the collective consciousness of what is good does not cause incongruence to those who choose to pass on hate to the next generation?

Researchers' Reflection: Fredah Mainah, PhD

Plurilingualism: Challenges of Speaking with a Recognizable "Non-Native" Accent

I fluently speak and write in three languages, and I have a basic experience of taking classes in German, Spanish, and French. I grew up in Kenya as a child of two worlds: city and village. While in the village, we spoke one native language that was common for all members of the community. In the city, however, it was a different case. Our neighbors and playmates were from all over the country and of different ethnic groups and as such spoke many different languages and dialects from our own. Our country has over 70 different ethnic groups, each with its own spoken language. To ease our communication, we created our own language, which was a mixture of English, Kiswahili, and our own native languages. Today, it has become a national language called Sheng.

At the community school, we were encouraged (a polite way of saying coercion and punishment) to speak in English both in class and outside. The punishment included physical lashes and being given a necklace with a wooden image of a donkey to wear as a deterrent. We called it *monito*, from the word "monitoring." To speak in English all day at school was a difficult task, and so we still found ourselves mixing two languages to communicate. The whipping from parents and insistence that we speak these foreign languages so that we can excel in the new world also made it worse. Culture, language assimilation, and immersion were not done in the foreign land but in the native land and the enforcers were native teachers and sometimes parents. Today, most citizens in former colonial countries do not speak their native languages especially while in school or in formal gatherings.

I remember one English class where the teacher asked us to compose sentences using the question word *Why*. In our native language, a similar sounding word exists (*whaii*), and it means "last night." It was no surprise therefore to hear sentences constructed based on that meaning. One example that comes to mind was a classmate who constructed his sentence, saying, "*Whaii* we ate cornbread."

Simplistic as this example might sound, the difficulty of communicating using a foreign language is more complex. Most times I feel as if I am an overloaded computer processing data before coming up with a sensible sentence either in response to a colleague's simple greeting or to a question in a staff or team meeting. Linguistic and cultural differences including lack of appropriate lexical and content knowledge of the target or named language to maintain fluency can complicate the process of communication. To a multilingual or plurilingual, however, the process can cause anxiety to the extent of causing self-doubt.

In a meeting, for example, I might sound as if I am stammering as I process my thoughts, switch between codes and translate some context that does not exist in English before finally speaking. To another who has not experienced the challenges of using a foreign language, they might just dismiss me or conclude that I had no idea what I was talking about or that I did not prepare for the meeting. In a casual or social conversation,

I might actually pause, not to think and construct, but to select from a list of languages. When we speak in native environments, we select a language depending on the person with whom we are speaking. If I am speaking to a person from my ethnic group, I may choose to use our native language as the base. If they are educated, I might use English as the base, and if they are not educated or not from my ethnic community, I might use Kiswahili. If it is a friend with whom I grew up, it will definitely be Sheng, where we switch codes among all the three languages.

After I speak, how am I then expected to respond to a supposed compliment that references my being smart and my voice being soothing? Do I take offense at the condescending tone I hear and the undertone of patronizing racism, or do I swallow my bottled-up anger and thank the benevolent colleague? Is it an innocent remark, or is it passive-aggressive hostility as the colleague soothes their own ego that was barely bruised when I sounded smart and professional and did not fit into the cookie cutter image of angry Black women?

Speaking in a foreign language requires one to have studied the language in depth so as to understand the rules of grammar, lexicon, and syntax, as well as nuances that are embedded in the slang, culture, and myths that are not part of the formal rules and class text. English is especially a very challenging language to learn. Its history reveals a lot of borrowed words and meanings from various European groups. For a learner of English as a foreign language who has no historical background knowledge, it becomes even more complex when they encounter words borrowed from French, Greek, German, or Latin.

I get asked a lot if these days I dream in English or my native language. Because of years of using the language, one becomes more used to thinking in it and eventually it becomes the dominant language for all functions.

Teaching in a predominantly Eurocentric class in the United States is scary sometimes. I have had students correct my pronunciation without the understanding that I was using a British spelling and pronunciation influenced by the British colonial legacy of my country of origin. I have also had experiences where the effort and time I have put into learning English is discounted and a demand is put on me to speak better. Speaking better, I later came to understand, meant speaking with an American accent!

Codes and switching in and out of different languages is a major characteristic and style of communication for plurilinguals. Overlay of languages in your brain, say French, English, Kiswahili, and other native languages, causes a delay in processing content and responses for ease of communication so much so that one may sound like one is not competent in the main language of the dominant culture. It is like a short circuit in radio communication, where there is a signal interference causing inability to fine-tune a channel to pick up the information needed for coherence and conversing. Yet the same communicator, given an individualized task to perform, can competently use the same dominant language to negotiate identity and demonstrate excellent use of the same said language both in speech and in writing. Online learning is a great example of this.

The authors' reflections and lived experiences shared above, as well as literature that was reviewed, demonstrate situations similar to those of the respondents, as shown in the sampled responses woven into the discussion. More challenges were identified concerning linguistic and cultural translations while speaking. Certain terms and concepts may not exist in other languages, or may have additional connotations that back translations do not always reveal. Challenges arise because of not only the content of word-for-word, literal translation, but the linguistic form of the language, such as tone, syntax, manner of questions posed, and so on.

Colonial legacy still has its effect on Africa. Centuries after they seemingly left, the impact of exploited natural resources, continued struggle in the previously colonized African countries, and the mental health effects inherited from generations that were subjected to all kinds of physical, mental, and psychological exploitation and alienation is still evident. Moreover, they were subjected to forced labor and were drafted to fight on the side of their colonial powers during World War I and World War II. My (Konaté) paternal father was captured by the Germans during World War II and was treated so poorly that he got frostbite in both of his feet. They had to amputate his big toes in both feet so that he could survive.

Colonized Africans were expected to look down on their own cultures and languages and to adopt Western languages, values, and worldviews. They had to assimilate to European languages, cultures, values, and religions, and devalue and abhor their own. To carry out their civilizing mission in Africa, European colonial powers used what the late British historian Basil Davidson (1994) refers to as the "Bible and the gun." The Bible symbolizes the process of the spiritual alienation of colonized Africans. Europeans looked down on African indigenous religions. They portrayed Africans as heathens and adopted Rudyard Kipling's (1899) claim of the "White Man's Burden" to justify their civilizing mission on the African continent. The gun embodies the brutality with which European colonial powers carried out their imperialistic endeavors on the African continent. Contrary to the narratives Europeans spun, that Africans happily welcomed European saviors without putting up any armed resistance and happily accepted European domination, the majority of Africans fought back against the loss of their freedom and the brutal occupation of their lands.

In the next chapter, the authors will discuss success by exploring literature and dimensions of success and human development as used by the United Nations Development Programme (UNDP), the Organisation for Economic Co-operation and Development (OECD), and the International Labour Organisation (ILO).

References

Council of Europe. 2001. *Common European Framework of Reference for Languages: Learning, Teaching, and Assessment*. Strasbourg: Language Policy Division. https://rm.coe.int/1680459f97.

Council of Europe. 2007. *Guide for the Development of Language Education Policies in Europe. From Linguistic Diversity to Plurilingual Education*. Main Version Draft. Strasbourg: Council of Europe. Language Policy Division. http://www.coe.int/t/dg4/linguistic/Source/FullGuide_EN.pdf.

Craythorne, Jennifer Laura. 2006. "Assimilating to Black America: How the Identity Choices of Haitian Immigrant and Haitian-American Students Are Impacted by Racial and Economic Segregation." PhD dissertation, University of Florida.

Davidson, Basil. 1994. *Modern Africa: A Social and Political History*. New York: Routledge.

Derwing, Tracey M., and Murray J. Munro. 2009. "Putting Accent in Its Place: Rethinking Obstacles to Communication." *Language Teaching* 42, no. 4: 476–90. https://doi.org/10.1017/S026144480800551X.

Diop, C. A. 1991. *Civilization or Barbarism*. Chicago: Chicago Review Press.

García, Ofelia and Ricardo Otheguy. 2019. "Plurilingualism and Translanguaging: Commonalities and Divergences." *International Journal of Bilingual Education and Bilingualism* 23, no. 1: 17–35.

Halagao, Patricia Espiritu. 2017. "Equity in Learning: Meeting the Needs of Multilingual Students in Hawai'i." *Kappa Delta Pi Record* 53, no. 2: 91–94.

Hecht, Michael L., Jennifer R. Warren, Eura Jung, and Janice L. Krieger. 2005. "A Communication Theory of Identity: Development, Theoretical Perspective, and Future Directions." In *Theorizing about Intercultural Communication*, edited by W. B. Gudykunst, 257–78. Thousand Oaks, CA: Sage.

Johnson, Rommel. 2019. "Negotiating American Racial Constructs: First-Generation African Caribbean Immigrants' Experience with Race." PhD dissertation, Western Michigan University.

Kalua, F. A. 2020. *Re-imagining African Identity in the Twenty-First Century: The Force of Intermediality*. Cambridge Scholars Publishing.

Karam, Fares J. 2018. "Language and Identity Construction: The Case of a Refugee Digital Bricoleur." *Journal of Adolescent & Adult Literacy* 61, no. 5: 511–21. https://doi.org/10.1002/jaal.719.

Schotte, Kristin, Petra Stanat, and Aileen Edele. 2017. "Is Integration Always Most Adaptive? The Role of Cultural Identity in Academic Achievement and in Psychological Adaptation of Immigrant Students in Germany." *Journal of Youth and Adolescence* 47, no. 1: 16–37.

Waters, Mary C. and Tomás R. Jiménez. 2005. "Assessing Immigrant Assimilation: New Empirical and Theoretical Challenges." *Annual Review of Sociology* 31, no. 1: 105–25.

Chapter 4

PERCEPTION AND DEFINITION
OF SUCCESS

In Chapter 4, the authors further discuss the issues of identity by exploring how sub-Saharan African immigrants perceive and define success. The major reason cited for immigrating was education, which was also perceived as a definition as well as a criterion of success.

Analogies have a way of expressing thoughts that the plain word cannot. The common analogy related to success in a hierarchical place like the United States is that of "pulling oneself up by the bootstraps" and having a strong work ethic. This is not only a contradiction in terms, as it is impossible to raise oneself by tugging on the loops of one's boots, but also a myth given the many systemic barriers that make it difficult for some groups to succeed, no matter how hard they work. The idiom incorrectly presupposes that we are all given the same chances on a level playing field and the environment is the same for all, that we all start at the same point, as in a race, and end at the same place called the "finishing line." The huge responsibility placed on the individual and the multitudes of factors that the individual has no control over are totally disregarded. It is like expecting someone to pull themselves out of a six-foot hole without any assistance. If the person succeeds, there is usually no recognition and appreciation for managing such a feat, especially if they belong to any of the minoritized groups. At the same time, factors and privileges extended to some individuals in the dominant group that allow them to thrive are downplayed.

Conditions for human development may be explored from a psychological approach and might include dimensions such as physical, biological, and cultural, as well as individual and social potentials and the immediate and external environment and their influences. Gone are the days when nations used to be measured by gross domestic product (GDP) and gross national product. These days even the bottom line has been replaced by the triple bottom line. Human development and well-being have been incorporated into the index of assessing a nation's success.

The United Nations Development Programme (UNDP) understands human development as "expanding the richness of human life" (UNDP n.d.a.). The approach goes beyond simple measures of the richness of an economy. Instead, the UNDP's human development approach looks at people's lives, their opportunities to gain skills and use those skills, and to have choices in how they fulfill their potential. The UNDP uses the Human Development Index (HDI) to measure three critical areas of growth: a long and healthy life, access to knowledge and a decent standard of living (UNDP n.d.b.). The HDI is adjusted by the inequality-adjusted HDI, Gender Development Index, Gender Inequality Index, and Multidimensional Poverty Index (UNDP 2020).

The UNDP's Human Development Report of 2020 describes GDP as a "crude indicator of economic achievements" (Baumann 2020). The report emphasizes human development for everyone and reformed global governance from an approach of individual agency and human freedoms, tolerance and the realization of the full potential of every human life presently alive and future generations. In this report, there is an emphasis on education for all and gender equity as well easing global pressures than in other reports.

From this approach, defining human development, well-being and success is a complicated process given the inequalities that exist between nations, as well as all the individual differences and all the global pressures. Human development is therefore considered as a composite of the factors that are involved in the shaping and development of human personality, sense of self and self-worth, moral development, decision-making and judgment, identity, agency and autonomy, behaviors, traits, life skills, social interactions, a broad worldview (as opposed to narrow identities and worldviews) and all characteristics whose interplay defines an individual's potential throughout their life span.

This definition of human development and success has evolved since the time of ancient philosophers who defined it along the dimensions of liberty (freedom to think freely), fraternity (access to common resources), and equality (fair treatment, justice, and institutions of governance that define and enforce justice, fairness, and opportunity for all). The UNDP 2020 Report also emphasizes issues of identity and its influence on agency and autonomy. It argues that people should have the liberty of choosing their identities among different identities that they value. The authors of the report conclude that it is important to recognize and respect such options because in the long term they have been demonstrated to be critical preconditions for peaceful coexistence (in its absence, extremism, and violence dominate) in a world that is increasingly becoming multiethnic, global, and borderless due to the coexistence of multicultural societies.

From the foregoing definitions and discussion about success and human development, the concept of identity is central to who we are and how we define ourselves, our worth and success. It is equally important to the ways in which others not only define us, but also the way they see and relate to us. For many immigrants, creating a sense of community and belonging in their host countries becomes necessary not just as a definition of identity but also for survival. Since they have left their families, cultures, religions, support system and way of life behind, they belabor to recreate them in their new environment.

However, many immigrants quickly realize the countless issues and dilemmas that arise when settling in a foreign country. For instance, several of our participants are torn between the desire to keep their original cultures and the pressures to assimilate to their new realities. Further, their experiences with racism and discrimination makes that internal struggle even more dire and complicated. According to the research of the Book Project Collective (2015, 113) on sub-Saharan African immigrants in Canada, "Factors such as family structures, self-knowledge, community support and social networks, employment, economic opportunities, a person's ability to cope with change, and the host society's acceptance of cultural diversity further complicate and impact identity negotiations." They go on to say that "the search for belonging and finding one's place is an ongoing process for immigrants of color, including those who are second and third generation. Linguistic ability is often used as a marker by those from one's culture of origin, as well as by Canadian society, to establish legitimate membership in a particular group" (Book Project Collective 2015, 113).

In their 2014 book titled, *The Triple Package: How Three Unlikely Traits Explain the Rise and Fall of Cultural Groups in America*, Amy Chua and Jed Rubenfeld explore the concept of success and the different ways in which immigrant communities harness its potency to their advantage or to their downfall. The authors argue that there are "three distinct forces," which are the combination of superiority, insecurity, and impulse control. They see all overachieving groups in the United States as connected by "three cultural commonalities" that they refer to as "the Triple Package," which is a catalyst for empowerment and one's drive towards success (Chua and Rubenfeld 2014). It determines why some immigrant groups who came from very humble beginnings succeed in America, while their peers from the same background and with the same abilities and opportunities do not.

Furthermore, Chua and Rubenfeld (2014, 1–2) state that, "successful people tend to feel simultaneously inadequate and superior. Certain groups tend to make their members feel this way more than others; groups that do so are disproportionately successful. This unlikely combination of qualities is part of a potent cultural package that generates drive: a need to prove oneself that makes people systematically sacrifice present gratification in pursuit of future attainment. Groups that instill this kind of drive in their members have a special advantage in America, because contemporary American culture teaches a contrary message- a message of self-acceptance and living in the moment." This is found commonly in the dominant cultures and in some sub-Saharan Africans who arrive confident in their goals.

According to Chua and Rubenfeld (2014), immigrants from many West Indian and African countries, such as Jamaica, Haiti, Ghana, Ethiopia and Liberia, are climbing America's higher education ladder, but that the most prominent are Nigerians. Nigerian Americans, most of them raised by immigrant parents, comprise a mere 0.7 percent of the United States Black population, yet this group accounts for at least ten times that percentage of Black students at America's most elite universities and professional schools (Chua and Rubenfeld 2014). Predictably, this academic success has translated into economic success. Nigerian Americans are already markedly overrepresented at Wall Street investment banks and blue-chip law firms (Chua and Rubenfeld 2014, 6–7).

The United States Census Report of 2017 (National Populations Projections), the American Community Survey in the New American Economy (2018) and Migration Policy Institute (2018) acknowledge that there has been comparatively little research on African immigrants and that sub-Saharan African immigrants hardly receive media attention, thus almost making them an "Invisible Model Minority." The reason posited as to why so little attention has been given to the sub-Saharan African immigrants is because their population is relatively small and because substantial African immigration to the United States is a recent phenomenon. Yet, in the same breath, these reports indicate that the influence of the sub-Saharan African immigrant population appears to be growing and the people who qualified to naturalize did so at high rates.

Despite the African immigration population in the United States remaining statistically lower compared to other immigrant populations (Logan and Deane 2003), its recent rise is attributed to the United States policy on family reunification, humanitarian policies for refugees and asylees and the Diversity Visa lottery program of 1990.

According to the Migration Policy Institute of 2018, the 2.1 million sub-Saharan African immigrants in the United States seem to settle in urban and suburban cities seeking communities that have other sub-Saharan African immigrants. Little Ethiopia in Los Angeles, California and Little Senegal in New York City are good examples. Sub-Saharan African immigrants also settle in some of the sanctuary/safe states. Most of the areas where there are concentrated settlements of sub-Saharan African immigrants have their own pluralistic religious meeting spaces led in their indigenous languages, as well as entrepreneurial nonprofit organizations, organizations resembling civic centers, their own grocery stores, ethnic restaurants, social support circles (for weddings, medical, funerals, and such) and medical clinics, thus creating unique African cultures in the United States.

When sub-Saharan African immigrants settle in states, they contribute to the local and national economies. According to a report by the New American Economy (2018, 17), in 2015, sub-Saharan African immigrants held $40.3 billion in spending power and contributed $14.8 billion in tax revenue. Household incomes of sub-Saharan African immigrants were the highest in California ($6.6 billion) and Texas ($6.3 billion), followed by Maryland ($5.6 billion), New York ($4.9 billion), Georgia and Virginia ($2.9 billion), and New Jersey ($2.5 billion) (New American Economy 2018, 6). As a result, those populations paid taxes ranging from $2 billion in California to $691 million in New Jersey. In addition, 38 percent of the naturalized sub-Saharan African immigrants from this growing population voted in the 2014 election (New American Economy 2018, 16).

To return to Chua and Rubenfeld's (2014) Triple Package, in their analysis of immigrant populations' drive to success, the authors link feelings of inadequacy to the insecurity that many immigrants feel. This insecurity is characterized by a feeling of not being good enough and not being valued, as well as a heightened anxiety and fear about losing everything. Chua and Rubenfeld's research shows that immigrant groups that have been able to harness their feeling of inadequacy as an impetus for drive, hard work, and determination are the most successful ones. Some of our respondents expressed the constant feeling of insecurity as immigrants in a foreign land:

I think as you grow older, like now I am worried about what do I have in Africa, do I have land?
I think it has both ways. It has been barrier for some things and for other things it has been positive. Then in other places in America, doesn't matter whether you are from Africa or not, you are Black. If you are from Africa, you worry about all the things that could affect your chances of accomplishing the goals you want to in this country, especially before you get your papers.

As far as the superiority complex element of the Triple Package is concerned, Chua and Rubenfeld (2014, 8) define it as "a deeply internalized belief in your group's specialness, exceptionality, or superiority." They further describe the superiority complex as "providing a kind of psychological armor of special importance to minorities who repeatedly face hostility and prejudice" (Chua and Rubenfeld 2014, 15). The authors elaborate, "Fending off majority ethnocentrism with their own ethnocentrism is a common strategy among successful minorities" (Chua and Rubenfeld 2014, 15). Indeed, some of our respondents reported being compelled by this complex and attributed their success in the United States to it:

> As a fact coming from outside the United States clearly has put one in a situation to always fall back on your African cultural background to push forward and so as immigrants you have this push and pull. One you have relatives at home that you need to take care of financially and otherwise so you are forced to sometimes take jobs that you ordinarily would not do but with hoping that those kinds of jobs are only temporary and you need to use that as a stepping step to bigger things.
> I am a person who knows how to build and maintain relationships. Since we are in a place that is globalized, everyone wants to make sure that they connect with people. It may not be the same for original born Americans because they have the individualistic attitude that they do not connect beyond that. I am very proud that my origin has contributed to my success. I adapted my mentality to that of this country and I didn't expect anyone to give me anything.
> I think what really pushed me was that I wanted to prove to the French people that you can go to another country, learn a different language and succeed; that was a great motivation to me when I came. Immigrants have a big problem, when you come to a new country either you adapt to it or you won't succeed.

Finally, the third component of the Triple Package is impulse control. The authors of this book repeatedly see participants expressing this characteristic. According to Chua and Rubenfeld (2014, 10), impulse control "refers to the ability to resist temptation, especially the temptation to give up in the face of hardship or quit instead of persevering at a difficult task." Chua and Rubenfeld point out the fact that in a society where everyone is taught to live in the moment, delaying gratification is not seen as very appealing. Yet, it is the application of a rigorous discipline, the power of enduring hardships and the ability to control the urges of instant gratification that fuel immigrant groups' success. Delayed gratification has been used successfully by some of our respondents as a technique to achieve success:

> Yes, one Kenyan lady. She came here with a great mind and had family support from her daughter and son. Her secret of success was

perseverance and always looking for opportunities. She was able to humble herself as she was well educated and had a very accomplished past. I came to America, as a sportsman and I realized I had much to learn and had to improve my life [...]. I went back to Uganda and when I did, I had a chance to come back. I travelled three to four times before I settled.

One participant's definition and practice of success is notable for demonstrating the resilience and determination to achieve success, a characteristic that many immigrants share. With regards to education as an achievement, as well as a criterion for success, he states:

To me success basically means never giving up and working towards achieving one's goals. I may not achieve success in one shot, or in the ways that I thought but if I eventually get there, then that is success for me. It doesn't mean that I will never fail, I must stop and rethink and redirect my energies and get focused again to get to that which I want to achieve. For me right now, success would be completing my PhD. That is huge for me right now.

According to Chua and Rubenfeld (2014, 3), "The Triple Package is accessible to anyone. It's a set of values and beliefs, habits and practices that individual from any background can make a part of their lives or their children's lives, enabling them to pursue success as they define it." However, the authors underscore the fact that the Triple Package forces run counter to the core principles of American culture. They explain that the complex of superiority is not acknowledged in a society that is built on the ideal of the equality of all. From research and lived experience, the authors of this book maintain that this statement is an overgeneralized interpretation because racism and White supremacy have been part and parcel of the United States since its inception. The concept of the "White Man's Burden" and "Manifest Destiny" that were used by European colonizers to dispossess and exterminate Native Americans and enslave and dehumanize Africans were both premised on the concept of the superiority of the White "race."

Nevertheless, it is undeniable that many immigrant groups do use their own sense of pride either in their religious background or ancestry to counter any sense of discrimination that they might experience in the United States. Indeed, Chua and Rubenfeld (2014, 11) state, "Because all three elements of the Triple Package run so counter to modern American culture, it makes sense that America's successful groups are all outsiders in one way or another. It also makes sense that so many immigrant communities are pockets of exceptional upward mobility in an increasingly stratified American economy."

In our research we asked our respondents a few questions on success. What we envisioned was to gather their perspectives to help us understand their perception of success, the expectations, and goals that their family set for them. Further we wanted to gauge how they measured success by asking about their observations of other African immigrants and their attempts at achieving success. The statements below are samples of their responses:

On what success is:

Success is when one is content with who they are, so they can be who they need to be. Success is always learning, always challenging myself and my surroundings.

Success to me means being able to live out your full potential in all facets of life including professional, family, financial and health, with the end goal of being able to help others and uplift society.

Happiness to me does not mean money but it means am I able to relate with people in a good way? Am I able to self- sustain myself? Am I able to enjoy life? Am I secure? Am I positive? I am a very positive minded person that I look at negatives as opportunities,

I think for me, success in America means to be able to support myself and my family back home, that is what I call success. I think as you grow older, like now I am worried about what do I have in Africa, do I have land? Really success is what I have achieved back home and less of what I have achieved in the United States. Our status back home is you have land, you have a house, you know that is achievement.

I think success is a very relative term, everyone is successful and if you set a goal. I think at least the way I look at it, success is not the destination, it is a progressive set goal. Any goal you set and do you are successful. If you set a goal to get a degree and you get it, you are successful, but you have to keep setting goals.

Success is more than just personal enrichment. To me, success is being able to impact the society, I was raised in a society where everything is lineal? So, until I share my personal achievements that is when I will feel like I am successful.

Being healthy, getting an education, working hard and having a family, support my family back home, retire back home, invest back home and in the US, starting my own business venture, being solid financially, having great relationships, and helping others, not let a million dollars get into my head, doing what I want to do, freedom, and enjoying it, being independent and happy, position myself to be a person of influence.

Others said:

> Success to me is being able to reach maximum potential using the unlimited resources available not excluding human resources to support yourself and family with no strain.

On how to achieve success, one respondent said:

> For me, I think success to me is seeing my kids become, go to school, get a job and do well in America. The fact that we are from Africa, we already have that determination and so I had no doubt that I would make it. The foundation was there, for me the way I am going to count success is if I see my three boys being successful in America, that is the way I am going to measure my success because I know I will be able to make it, because I have the determination. The atmosphere is different from Africa, different things going on for me success is going to be determined on how my boys do.

Another respondent stated that:

> I think everybody can be successful if you set goals and you achieve it. You know somebody who is high school and set goals to graduate is successful. Or another person who sets a goal to graduate college or professional school or whatever. If someone sets goal to achieve, they have to keep setting goals all your life, you shouldn't stop. When you stop, you stop being successful. That is how I see it.

Yet another said:

> I explain that, by I adapted my mentality to that of this country and I didn't expect anyone to give me anything. I tell my wife all the time, if you come here to sleep, go to bed, go back home. So, this country is not easy for sure, you have to be self-reliant and not on people which is a big difference between here and most other countries in the world basically. You have to must persevere, if you are an immigrant and you don't persevere, won't work.

Some respondents said that they set their own standards for success, and they incorporated family expectations:

> I set my own goals and my family too accept and support me in that. I have had to adjust my goals and the path towards my definition of

success. Not being able to make enough money to live on and support my family as much as I would like is hard

I was hoping to get education, a job and opportunities but being on my own and no social or economic support is hard

I set myself 1) to intellectually improve myself because I realized this is a [...] [couldn't make out what he said at 4:24] country. Then I also set myself to be self-sustained that I could do better using my talents, my education and use that to help my people back in Uganda. In totality, I looked at it as a total personal development to lead me to a higher sustainability. I can get what I can get and pass it on to other people, in any way it might not be money because things are different. I may not be able to give you money, but I can give you wisdom that could change your life. So that is how I look at it, those that are close to that I can give money too that's fine. Those that are close to me that I can give a word of wisdom because of my status and where I am, I believe that also is very wonderful. If someone gives you a word of cautionary wisdom and it changes your life it could be more than. Teachers don't give us money in school, but they give us knowledge so the knowledge makes us to be better.

One, I needed to go to school. Two, support my family back home. Three, be financially better than the way I was in Uganda. Those were the three things; my family will be better because I am here.

Other observations of successful Africans:

Graduated with the degrees they set out to get. Graduated on time. Proceeded to higher levels of education. Some got jobs with leading industries in their field, others got good jobs back in Kenya and had a good transition back into Kenya after years of being here.

I do not know any people but there are people around that I know are happy with what they have achieved, and I would say that they have reached their expectations in life.

Yes, I know many that have come here and been successful and I emulate them in one way or another to follow their path and to know how they have made it to the top. I make sure I outreach them, interact with them, ask them questions, ask for guidance, advice which they have totally given me. So, I could use those as lessons or experiences to better myself.

Actually, for Nigerians they are in different professions in the United States, and most are medical doctors.

Literature reviewed for this section indicates that although sub-Saharan African immigrants have a solid understanding of what they want in life and how to achieve it, there are other challenges in the United States for which they are unprepared. The role of integrating new students into higher education and into the community at large as immigrants is taken seriously, especially on campuses, by most professors, instructors, teachers, community leaders and career counselors. At many institutions of higher education, for example, there are resources and programs specifically for first-year and transfer students to ensure that those students get adequate support for their integration into university life. However, the specific needs of immigrants, for example, their particular challenges in adapting to life in a new country and the specific roadblocks they face in securing employment as non-US citizens, are generally not well cared for.

Shizha et al. (2020) found that the colonialized categorization of Blackness as unintelligent influences some academic counselors who consciously or unconsciously internalize that narrative and as a result counsel African immigrant learners as if they were unintelligent. Based on that prejudicial stereotype and having low expectations of students with darker skin tones, such counselors guide African immigrant learners toward career choices and pathways that lead them to lower-tier universities because of their ethnic background, not academic achievement. This type of counsel eventually leads students to courses of study that are not well suited for success on the job market. Despite the effort these immigrants put into adapting and assimilating, navigating multiple sociocultural environments and continents, as well as working hard to achieve success, they are not spared the institutionalized racism in the United States that treats people of color with disdain.

In their analysis of shifts in understanding in the nature of hard work as a pathway to success and freedom, Knight et al. (2016) highlight the role played by family expectations, education structures and the definition of the American dream. They found that racist beliefs about who achieves the dream, as well as negative schooling experiences, soon become a barrier to highly motivated and skilled African immigrants. Motivation and aspiration also start to decline once these immigrants realize that the negative dominant narratives about hard work, intelligence, meritorious performance, and success are applied to them by others whether those labels are warranted or not.

Knight et al. (2016) found that agency, self-will and determination cause sub-Saharan African immigrants to redefine the American dream and how to achieve it. Their dream is achieved by becoming self-fulfilled, working harder than the average American and standing out by gaining higher education levels and physical and spiritual achievements. Additionally, sub-Saharan African immigrants further achieve their American dreams by supporting their parents and relatives back in their native countries while dreaming of going back to their native countries when they have achieved overall well-being.

In their research into the ways that African immigrants cope with the challenges they encounter in their pursuit of the American dream, Kumi-Yeboah et al. (2020) focus on identity, civic engagement, education, social integration, acculturation strategies and academic experiences. They recommend that educational institutions, educators and policymakers make more effort to support African immigrant learners through integration, education success and assimilation programs. This support would go a long way in easing the challenges encountered, including dealing with negative dominant cultural narratives about African immigrants, their intelligence and work ethics, as well as the strain of social, cultural, and linguistic differences and the stress and fatigue caused by dealing with discrimination.

Definition and Perception of Success in Higher Education

Most of the respondents for this research came to the United States in search of higher education and other factors of success. Because of that, the authors reviewed literature to reconcile the responses and the experiences in higher education. Most literature argues that students' success and engagement in higher education should not be a focus and burden of the learner alone, given the increasingly complex academic expectations, economic, social, political, linguistic, and cultural issues they constantly face (Kuh et al. 2006; Vinson et al. 2010; Chua and Rubenfeld 2015; Shizha et al. 2020).

These researchers as discussed above, defined student success as those purposeful academic activities that result in students' satisfaction, acquisition and attainment of educational and personal objectives that have a utility level beyond college. Their methodology included student success measures and outcomes, such as satisfaction with experiences and how comfortable and affirmed students felt in a learning environment. Moreover, they discussed how pedagogies and technology used for facilitating learning contribute to student success. They emphasized the importance of "becoming proficient in writing, speaking, critical thinking, scientific literacy, quantitative skills, and more highly developed levels of personal functioning represented by self-awareness, confidence, self-worth, social competence, and sense of purpose" (Kuh et al. 2006, 5).

Arguing for student engagement and smooth transitions as a key component of student success, Vinson et al. (2010) suggest that the background of a student, their social and personal lived experiences, should always be considered when programming for higher education. Individual behaviors and higher education conditions and factors, including "encouraging cooperation between students, encouraging active learning and encouraging contact between students and staff" were cited as major engagement indicators (132).

Although the study above focuses on United States students, not international students, it nonetheless highlights some issues that cut across all students in higher education. Among the many issues that most students face in higher education are failure to complete their program, funding and access to student loans, student housing, lack of academic support and resources, such as counseling, and the rising cost both of living and of higher education. The situation for international students is more complex because of complications presented by immigration laws and the expectations and pressures from their families, as discussed in this chapter and Chapter 7 on the "myth of going back home."

Persistence and completion issues always plague sub-Saharan African immigrants. This is compounded by external factors related to legal immigration and higher education requirements. Students, for example, are confronted with issues ranging from higher course load and the higher tuition fees, to the exorbitant price of student housing, and the complexity of legal work (which must occur on campus unless one has a scholarship, has graduated or is on Optional Practical Training).

Dropping out due to lack of funds was cited by the student respondents of this research as the main reason for not successfully completing their degree and achieving success. Some argued that if they had a better paying job on campus, they could have subsidized what their sponsors were paying and not fallen behind. This was especially true when tuition fees and student housing costs rose to a level that the sponsor had not anticipated.

For a local student, dropping out could mean taking on multiple low-paying jobs to survive. For an international student, it almost always means going back home or taking the risk of working under the table. If immigration catches up with them, then deportation and a possible immigration bar are the consequences. These hurdles are not easy to overcome. For each international student drop out, regardless of each person's unique circumstances, consider the waste in terms of the time and money initially invested and the long-term loss, including the emotional burden on the student. Teaching excellence, research, mentoring and coaching, and grant writing were factors that were considered when evaluating the success of professors in higher education, but student engagement was not among those dimensions of measurement. From this research, this omission seems to be a huge gap, as engagement has increasingly been recognized as a critical component of student success in terms of retention and graduation.

The authors further explored how each gender defines success. Our phenomenological study revealed that male respondents felt more pressure to succeed when they go abroad for further studies. The pressure came from the immediate family and the community as well. Male respondents stated that they felt the pressure of completing their degrees and getting jobs to earn not only a livelihood for themselves but also for the sake of their parents and the community. Their feelings reflect the reality that the definition of success in their native countries was extended to the community. Indeed, parents' success is assessed by the success of their children, especially the male.

Further, the male respondents reported feeling pressure to get married if they were single. Students in most United States universities are not allowed to work off campus, yet these male respondents are expected to support families back home as well as get married and support their own nuclear families. In addition, they had to pay their tuition at international students' rates. A semester of academic work brings its own pressure, with full-time enrollment being an average 12 credit hours. If a student does not have financial support from their native country and does not manage to get a scholarship or a campus job that includes a tuition subsidy, the likelihood of falling behind academically and economically rises significantly.

On average, most international students who were interviewed for this research, worked on campus, earning barely enough for food and accommodation. Those who were lucky enough to get a tuition subsidy were also under more pressure to excel academically or lose the subsidy. A subsidy is not full tuition, so the student still needs to work an extra job to cover the difference. It is therefore not surprising to find an international student, regardless of where they come from, struggling to work multiple jobs, including off-campus jobs, to cover their expenses.

Some students find solutions to all these issues by marrying United States citizens. With a marriage certificate, they can now work off campus legally. However, those marriages often bring their own kind of pressure and cultural clashes. In many communities of sub-Saharan Africa, male traditional roles do not include household chores such as cooking, cleaning, babysitting, laundry and so on. Household chores are usually regarded as the domain of female gender roles. In some American households, chores are shared differently and may depend on who is home to do those chores. In addition, roles may shift over time. The reality of the blurring those roles when the sub-Saharan African males emigrate to the United States, start a family there, and find they are expected to cook, change diapers, clean, and do other household chores may result in additional pressure due to role shifting and culture conflicts.

Moreover, those students cannot get their dream jobs since they are still in school, and so they take the available menial jobs with low pay. These kinds of pressures result in identity crises and role conflict. They may experience dissonance and incongruence management because they feel demeaned and are ashamed to do household chores while working at low-paying jobs that also causes them to underperform at college, thus further compounding the goal of educational and career success. Some sub-Saharan African immigrants came to the United States as educated and skilled workers, such as veterinarians and teachers, yet they could not get jobs in their fields and so took minimum wage jobs in retail, farm work, construction or as health aides just to keep up the dream.

Some of the male respondents admitted to having divorced their anchor wives after getting their Green Card (legal status) because they could not cope with being husbands and students. However, given all these pressures, some fell so behind in college that they were reported by their universities to the immigration department and eventually were deported. Those who persevered in their marriages and in college admitted that eventually the success they now enjoy made it all worth it.

One other male who was interviewed for this study stated that he had almost finished his veterinary degree in his native country when he decided to come to the United States to complete the degree and get a different perspective as well as hands-on experience. Unfortunately, the registrar's office at the United States university changed the entrance requirements for the degree program to which he had been admitted. The result was that he was required to take some undergraduate prerequisites that had not been included in his original budget. Just a few more classes completely derailed his plan.

In the meantime, he fell in love with a female United States citizen. He said that his relationship was not for his legal status, but it was hard convincing the immigration department otherwise. Although eventually he got his Green Card, he was frustrated that just because he is a foreigner, his love was not recognized as such but only treated as an economic transaction. Further frustration came when he tried to get a job as a veterinarian, and he could only get minimum wage jobs on farms assisting farmers and not at a clinic where he was trained to work.

Yet another male respondent had come to the United States with his wife to complete their PhDs. Because of role and culture conflicts, they eventually got divorced. Back home in their native country, it was easy for the woman to conform to that culture and its expectations. In the United States, the female had observed that some men help their wives with household chores because both of them work or are in college. When the African male does not conform to the new norms, pressure builds in the marriage, and divorce becomes the eventual solution.

In our analysis we found some recurring characteristics that were common to those male students who persevered and adapted to their United States environment much faster than others, eventually bringing them success. These included resilience, self-efficacy, hope, optimism and self-discipline; strong social support from their native country, personal relationships and interpersonal skills; and the role of religion and spirituality as variables of resilience, issues of identity and belonging.

Responses by the female respondents differed only in the perspective of gender roles and the pressure of living in two worlds more so than the specifics of getting jobs and working through heavy higher education course work and schedules. Their identity issues were more complex than the male respondents and will be discussed separately under the ideological and psychological motivations in Chapter 6.

Literature reviewed for this chapter corresponded with the respondents' views in terms of personal and national identity, self-worth, the value of education and defining and achieving success. According to UNDP, those who emigrated to the United States demonstrated a sense of individual agency, autonomy, and self-determination. The UNDP adds that individuals develop such features by expanding their worldview, choosing how they want to experience life, defining their self-worth and self-respect and creating a sense of community and belonging. Additionally, individuals who emigrated develop agency, autonomy, and self-determination by getting educated in the areas of their interest to enjoy a decent standard of living that could lead to a long and healthy life in the context of political freedom, good governance, fairness, and justice.

References

Adepoju, Adunola. 2004. "Feminisation of Poverty in Nigerian Cities: Insights from Focus Group Discussions and Participatory Poverty Assessment." *African Population Studies*, 19: 141–54.

Baum, Sandy and Stella M. Flores. 2011. "Higher Education and Children in Immigrant Families." *The Future of Children* 21, no. 1: 171–93. doi:10.1353/foc.2011.0000.

Baumann, F. 2021. "The Next Frontier—Human Development and the Anthropocene: UNDP Human Development Report 2020. *Environment: Science and Policy for Sustainable Development* 63, no. 3: 34–40.

Carling, Jørgen and María Hernández-Carretero. 2011. "Protecting Europe and Protecting Migrants? Strategies for Managing Unauthorised Migration from Africa." *The British Journal of Politics and International Relations* 13, no. 1: 42–58.

Chua, Amy and Jed Rubenfeld. 2014. *The Triple Package: How Three Unlikely Traits Explain the Rise and Fall of Cultural Groups in America.* New York: Penguin Books.

Eastwood, J. B., R. E. Conroy, S. Naicker, P. A. West, R. C. Tutt, and J. Plange-Rhule. 2005. "Loss of Health Professionals from Sub-Saharan Africa: The Pivotal Role of the UK." *The Lancet* 365, no. 9474: 1893–900.

George Mwangi, Chrystal A., Nina Daoud, Alicia Peralta, and Sharon Fries-Britt. 2019. "Waking from the American Dream: Conceptualizing Racial Activism and Critical Consciousness among Black Immigrant College Students." *Journal of College Student Development* 60, no. 4: 401–20.

Hagopian, Amy, Anthony Ofosu, Adesegun Fatusi, Richard Biritwum, Ama Essel, L. Gary Hart, and Carolyn Watts. 2005. "The Flight of Physicians from West Africa: Views of African Physicians and Implications for Policy." *Social Science and Medicine* 61, no. 8: 1750–60.

Hatton, Timothy J. and Jeffrey G. Williamson. 2003. "Demographic and Economic Pressure on Emigration out of Africa." *Scandinavian Journal of Economics* 105, no. 3: 465–86.

Hecht, Michael L., Jennifer R. Warren, Eura Jung, and Janice L. Krieger. 2005. "A Communication Theory of Identity: Development, Theoretical Perspective, and Future Directions." In *Theorizing about Intercultural Communication*, edited by W. B. Gudykunst, 257–78. Thousand Oaks, CA: Sage.

Hoggart, Keith and Cristóbal Mendoza. 1999. "African Immigrant Workers in Spanish Agriculture." *Sociologia Ruralis* 39, no. 4: 538–62.

Kiramba, Lydiah Kananu, Adaurennaya C. Onyewuenyi, Alex Kumi-Yeboah, and Anthony Mawuli Sallar. 2020. "Navigating Multiple Worlds of Ghanaina-born Immigrant Adolescent Girls in US Urban Schools." *International Journal of Intercultural Relations* 77: 46–57.

Knight, Michelle G., Rachel Roegman, and Lisa Edstrom. 2016. "My American Dream: The Interplay between Structure and Agency in West African Immigrants' Educational Experiences in the United States." *Education and Urban Society* 48, no. 9: 827–51.

Kuh, George D., Jillian Kinzie, Jennifer A. Buckley, Brian K. Bridges and John C. Hayek. 2006. *What Matters to Student Success: A Review of the Literature*. Commissioned report for the National Symposium on Postsecondary Student Success: Spearheading a Dialog on Student Success. Washington, DC: National Postsecondary Education Cooperative.

Kumi-Yeboah, Alex, Gordon Brobbey and Patriann Smith. 2020. "Exploring Factors that Facilitate Acculturation Strategies and Academic Success of West African Immigrant Youth in Urban Schools." *Education and Urban Society* 52, no. 1: 21–50.

Logan, J. R., and G. Deane. 2003. *Black Diversity in Metropolitan America*. Lewis Mumford Center for Comparative Albany: Urban and Regional Research, University of Albany.

Luther, Rashmi., Vanaja Dhruvarajan, Ikram Ahmed Jama, Yumi Kotani, Monia Mazigh, Peruvemba S. Jaya and Lucya Spencer, eds. 2015. The Book Project Collective (*Resilience and Triumph: Immigrant Women Tell Their Stories*). Toronto: Second Story Press.

Massey, Douglas S. 1999. "International Migration at the Dawn of the Twenty-first Century: The Role of the State." *Population and Development Review* 25, no. 2: 303–22.

New American Economy. 2018. *Power of the Purse: How Sub-Saharan African Immigrants Contribute to the U.S. Economy*. January 2018. http://research.newamericaneconomy.org/wp-content/uploads/sites/2/2018/01/NAE_African_V6.pdf.

Owusu, Thomas Y. 1999. "Residential Patterns and Housing Choices of Ghanaian Immigrants in Toronto, Canada." *Housing Studies* 14, no. 1: 77–97.

Shizha, Edward, Ali A. Abdi, Stacey Wilson-Forsberg, and Oliver Masakure. 2020. "African Immigrant Students and Postsecondary Education in Canada: High School

Teachers and School Career Counsellors as Gatekeepers." *Canadian Ethnic Studies* 52, no. 3: 67–86.

UNDP (United Nations Development Programme). 2020. "Technical Notes: Calculating the Human Development Indices–Graphical Presentation." Accessed June 7, 2022. https://hdr.undp.org/sites/default/files/hdr2020_technical_notes.pdf.

———. n.d.a. "About Human Development." Accessed June 7, 2022. https://hdr.undp.org/en/humandev.

———. n.d.b. "Human Development Index." Accessed June 7, 2022. https://hdr.undp.org/en/content/human-development-index-hdi.

Vinson, Don, Sarah Nixon, Barbara Walsh, Cath Walker, Elizabeth Mitchell, and Elena Zaitseva. 2010. "Investigating the Relationship between Student Engagement and Transition." *Active Learning in Higher Education* 11, no. 2: 131–43.

Waters, Mary C. 2014. "Defining Difference: The Role of Immigrant Generation and Race in American and British Immigration Studies." *Ethnic and Racial Studies* 37, no. 1: 10–26.

Chapter 5

RACISM AND DISCRIMINATION

Our Nation derives strength from the diversity of its population and from its commitment to equal opportunity for all. We are at our best when we draw on the talents of all parts of our society, and our greatest accomplishments are achieved when diverse perspectives are brought to bear to overcome our greatest challenges.
    —President Obama, Executive Order 13583, Establishing a Coordinated Government-wide Initiative to Promote Diversity and Inclusion in the Federal Workforce, August 18, 2011

Chapter 5 delves deeper into the challenges of coming to the United States and being confronted with issues of race, national narratives adopted to describe all peoples of color and discrimination along color lines.

Sub-Saharan African immigrants may have familiarity with what it means to be discriminated against from their colonial history and the divide-and-rule strategy that resulted in what today is evident as ethnic conflicts. However, in their homelands, they have not been exposed to the kind of color-based racism they experience when they emigrate out of Africa. The kind of discrimination based on race that Black people have been subjected to since slavery is unique. The caste system (race hierarchies) in the United States is one of the most brutal and dehumanizing in the world.

The responses from the interviewees demonstrate clearly that sub-Saharan African immigrants know what discrimination is but are not very familiar with the kind of racism that is part and parcel of the racial hierarchy in the United States. At first, they view racism as a hindrance and challenge, before coming to the realization of its historical context and the magnitude of its impact on their lives. Resilience is one competency they use to devise coping mechanisms. One respondent says:

My experience in Nigeria would be that I have to confront ethnic discrimination. We have about 250 languages in Nigeria so that in itself is a different experience and then coming here I have never up to the time I came to North America, Canada and United States, I have never confronted racial discrimination in high school. I had Irish reverend fathers as my teachers, British council teachers, and American Peacecorp volunteers. The relationship was not on the basis of race. We were more in terms of what I can benefit from my teachers.

Another respondent compares and contrasts discrimination in Nigeria and in the United States in the following words:

Yes, there was ethnic discrimination. You might apply for a job in Nigeria and if you don't belong to the majority ethnic group you might not get the job but that is not to say that anybody puts you down to say you can't make it [...] but for African Americans they really don't have the choice.

As we can see from the responses discussed above, some of our respondents have encountered ethnic discrimination in their countries of origin, as well as racism in the United States. The various coping mechanisms they have devised to deal with racism and discrimination in the United States reflect their experiences not only as Black people, but also as newcomers in a foreign land. Other factors such as class, religion, nationality, and ethnicity of our respondents impacted both their experiences and the different ways in which they responded to its challenges. In order to understand the multifaceted experiences of sub-Saharan African immigrants in the United States, it is important to understand the concept of intersectionality and how multiple dimensions of identity affect and inform their coping strategies.

Intersectionality is the idea that different identities such as race, class, gender, nationality, culture, language, religion, sexuality, age, physical ability, and occupations work together to define and determine our experiences as individuals. People's unique experiences within a culture vary widely depending upon factors such as disability, age, sexual orientation, region, and religion. This interplay of these different social categories is referred to as "intersectionality." The concept of intersectionality as defined by Kimberley Crenshaw (1989) examines relationships and interactions between multiple axes of identity and multiple dimensions of social organization at the same time. Gender and race, for example, are intersectional because the way they are enacted and experienced depends on the way they interact with other social categories and identities. According to Thornton and Zambrane (2009, 176), intersectionality, as a framework for studying inequalities and oppression, is important because it "combines advocacy, analysis, theorizing, and pedagogy which are essential to the production of knowledge and the pursuit of social justice and equality." Intersectional scholarship is about understanding and explaining the lives and experiences of marginalized people and by examining the constraints and demands of the many structures that influence their options and opportunities (Thornton and Zambrane 2009, 178). As an analytical strategy, intersectionality may be used as a systematic approach to understanding human life and behavior that is rooted in the experiences and struggles of marginalized people.

As foreigners who live in the margins of American society, many sub-Saharan African immigrants are othered because their experiences are discounted since they are neither documented nor similar to those of the majority of Americans. According to Johnson et al. (2004, 253) "Othering is a process that identifies those that are thought to be different from oneself or the mainstream, and it can reinforce and reproduce positions of domination and subordination." Sub-Saharan African immigrants experience othering because they look and talk differently, because their worldview, cultures and values are different, and because other dimensions associated with their Blackness and immigration status are also different from those of most Americans. As a result of othering, institutionalized racism and discriminatory laws and regulations (redlining, police brutality, drug sentencing laws, toxic waste dumping into minoritized communities, etc.) position mainstream Americans as superior and more deserving of rights. At the same time, those same laws and regulations are used to justify inequality and discrimination based on superficial differences, and as such treat sub-Saharan African immigrants as inferior and undeserving.

One of our respondents shares his experiences with othering in the United States when an interviewer blatantly shared that they were searching for a White professor:

I went for a campus interview. After picking me up at the airport, the chair of the search committee and I were driving to the hotel and he just, you know I don't know why he did that, he just said you know what you know aah we were really looking for a White male, an older White male but aah sorry that is the situation. I was taken aback; I was asking myself why did you bring me to campus if you already made up your mind. (Interviewer: Exactly, I thought that was against the law). It is, but so right from the onset I knew that there was no hope of getting the job. At the end it did not get the White male that they were looking for. They ended up with an older White female Africanist.

Another respondent recounts their experience with accent:

I went into an interview and the interviewer who was supposed to be my boss at that time asked me a funny question she said "Do people ever tell you that you have an accent?" I looked at her and said yeah. She then asked, "What do you say to them?" I said that they have an accent too and she cracked up and said "that is a very good answer." I got that job, because she said when they say I cannot hear you as much and I tell them look at it this way you have your accent and I have mine. If I'm able to listen to you, you should be able to listen to someone else that you can hear them as well.

This respondent recounts their experience with religion:

For instance, I interviewed for a job as an assistant professorship in my early years at a university. It was not a campus interview, it was a conference interview and it was clear that because of religious beliefs system, when I spoke to the representative of the history department at the conference, I think it was America Historical Association conference, I don't remember the city now either it was Chicago or somewhere you know, he clearly (even though we had a good interview) he clearly said oh no you are not a Mormon so we cannot. I am sorry we won't hire you. Yeah because religious [...] have a right not to hire the people they don't want to hire.

Another respondent recounts their experience with gender and culture:

So it was a shield to be Senegalese in the US and being Black in the US I came across as interesting, people asked questions and social studies for them. Some people talk about the lion. Did lions walk around, you know silly questions but it was I think it was a shield. My gender, I tend to have a very strong personality and I have never been in the position where gender was in the way. If something needed to be said I said it. If a tone of voice needed to be adopted, I adopted it. I have been in situations where they are only men and I am the only woman but when I speak everybody listens. There was no choice otherwise. I do understand there are gender disparities, maybe insidious. I never felt personally like I was hindered because of who I was whether regarding my nationality or gender.

This respondent recounts their experience with nationality:

People kinda of give you a second chance just because you are from Africa, especially people who understand the struggles of Africa. They give you the opportunity to have a second chance.

Other respondents shared their struggle with tribalism:

> I sort of broaden my identity. I am Ethiopian and that heritage is important and I'm very non-tribal. Right now tribalism is a big issue in Ethiopia. Mesa's legacy was to divide the country into tribes. That is a problem in Ethiopia.
>
> What is creating problems is identity politics based on clans. Like Somalia, the same clan conflict, one clan saying they're superior because of dictatorship and so we need to manage.
>
> We can think of Rwanda two major ethnic groups Hutu and Tutsi commit genocide. What has happened, instead of calling themselves Rwandese they are calling themselves Hutu, Tutsi and Hutu are a majority.

Skewed perceptions about foreigners in general, and specifically as demonstrated by the abovementioned accounts of othering and discrimination, are some of the factors that cause sub-Saharan African immigrants to either assimilate and/or reconstruct their identities. Moreover, many of them devise coping strategies through the creation of religious organizations, grocery stores, and social and community support systems like parties and celebratory events, some of which are aligned with events in their countries of origin like Independence Day and other national events. Discrimination is not alien to the majority of sub-Saharan African immigrants who come from former colonial countries. To further explore the challenges of coming to the United States and being confronted with issues of race and discrimination along color lines, it is necessary to retrace the root causes of those prejudices.

Colonization and imperialism continue to impact Africa even in the twenty-first century, and despite years of resisting and establishing decolonializing initiatives, the forces of colonization and imperialism will continue to impact Africa unless a paradigm shift happens on a global level. Colonization is a process whereby a foreign country physically occupies another country and imposes political, economic, and cultural control over its people. The colonization of the African continent happened toward the end of the nineteenth century when several European colonial powers, France, Germany, Spain, Portugal, and Great Britain, met in Berlin, Germany, from 1884 to 1885 to share the African continent among themselves in order to avoid fighting over it. This came to be referred to as the "scramble" for Africa. Each European colonial power wanted to have the biggest slice of the African cake. The abovementioned European countries each established spheres of influence, and by the beginning of the twentieth century, the entire continent of Africa, except Ethiopia, was completely under European colonial occupation.

In the beginning of the twentieth century, European countries measured their power by the number of colonies that they owned. The more colonies a country had, the more powerful it appeared. European colonial powers moved their military into the African countries they had claimed and physically occupied them. They used their African colonies as cash cows to fuel and develop their own economies. They exploited the natural resources of their African colonies; exported the raw natural resources to fuel the industrial revolution; forced Africans to work for free to build roads, bridges, dams, airports, and houses for the colonialists; and forced Africans to fight each other, to help the colonialists subdue more Africans and annex more territories. They squashed any form of resistance with sheer brutality. They killed and maimed people, collected taxes without representation, and subdued African people to obedience using brutal force. They also drew manpower from their African colonies during World War I and World War II.

The European colonization of the African continent, although not an episodic event, lasted about 76 years, except for South Africa that eventually got its independence in 1994. Its impact was devastating (and continues to be) for Africans whose continent has been depleted of its natural resources and who have been killed and traumatized, forced to adopt Western cultures and languages, religions, and way of life, despite the fact that Africans were always seen as less than their European counterparts. European colonizers brainwashed Africans to look down on their cultures, and they falsified African history to make them feel inferior. Today this kind of violation of human rights would have been a major headline in all media outlets, and would probably make it to the International Court of Justice, but in those days the lack of mass communication techniques played to the colonizers' advantage.

Europeans had a negative and profound influence on Africans. They broke the closeness Africans had with nature and with each other. They equally ended the relation of gender interdependence that existed in indigenous African cultures. Europeans brought to Africa what Basil Davidson (1994) refers to as "Westernization without real modernization." According to Davidson, the West has given Africa only the glimmering illusion of industrial know-how in exchange for African resources that they have been squandering for centuries. He states that what Africans need is the ability to carry out real development themselves for their own benefit. Davidson (1994, https://www.youtube.com/watch?v=X75COneJ4w8) refers to the African continent as "God's treasure chest of diamonds" and as the "Golden continent." However, Europeans have introduced in Africa a technology that was very destructive and that sowed death and desolation. He points out the irony of a continent so rich in natural resources, but so stricken by poverty.

"Today we live in a world that is characterized by coloniality rather than colonialism" (Ndlovu 2018, 96). Colonization is understood from a Eurocentric perspective as the engine that "modernizes" and "civilizes" the so-called "barbaric" and "uncivilized" world. What Rudyard Kipling (1898) calls the "White Man's Burden" of "go in and put all the weight of your influence into hanging on permanently" aptly characterizes imperialism and neocolonialism. This philosophy is hideously operationalized through different kinds of institutional power via agencies such as the IMF, the World Bank, and other so-called development partners, as well as religious and non-government organizations.

Sabelo Ndlovu-Gatsheni defines decolonization as a very complex and expansive phenomenon, which has consequences that extend across planet earth. According to Ndlovu-Gatsheni, "colonialism is the desire for the colonialist to claim the earth as their own, to conquer the people, nature and all aspects of human life and subject them to colonial power" (Ndlovu-Gatsheni 2021). Colonization began in the fifteenth century. Ndlovu-Gatsheni further points out the simultaneity between decolonization and colonization due to the fact that African people resisted their oppression and colonization from the very beginning.

Ndlovu-Gatsheni goes on to say that decolonization is a complex phenomenon, which encompasses the concepts of coloniality of power, coloniality of knowledge, coloniality of being and decoloniality of the concept of "empty land or space." Its aim is to undo the impacts of colonialism. The subjugation of people to colonial powers, which scholars refer to as "the coloniality of being," is a process whereby people are ranked according to social and racial hierarchies. A second characteristic feature of coloniality of being, which Ndlovu-Gatsheni points out, is that it upholds and legitimizes knowledge to colonial power in such a way that knowledge from Europe and North America becomes the only valid knowledge. All other types of knowledge are marginalized. "Epistemology constitutes an overarching theory of knowledge. It investigates the standards used to assess knowledge or why we believe what we believe to be true. Far from being the apolitical study of truth, epistemology points to the ways in which power relations shape who is believed and why" (Collins 2010, 270). Thus decolonization seeks to free what Foucault (1980) calls, "subjugated knowledges" from the chains of Western colonial hegemony.

In his attempt to define coloniality and modernity, Ndlovu-Gatsheni (2019) describes the concept of coloniality as "the trans-historic expansion of colonial domination and the perpetuation of its effects in contemporary times." Decoloniality, he argues, is part of marginalized but persistent movements that emerged from struggles against the slave trade, imperialism, colonialism, apartheid, neo-colonialism and underdevelopment as constitutive negative elements of hegemonic Euromodernity. He defines decolonization/ decoloniality "as both a political and epistemological movement gesturing towards an attainment of ecologies of knowledges and pluriversality" (Ndlovu-Gatsheni 2019, 202–3).

He then goes on to argue that decolonization/decoloniality poses "the challenges the present globalization and its pretensions of universalism, which hides the reality of the Europeanization and Americanization of the modern world" (Ndlovu-Gatsheni 2019, 202–3). Mignolo's (2007, 39) argument relates these definitions to each other: "'Modernity' is a European narrative that hides its darker side, 'coloniality'. Coloniality, in other words, is constitutive of modernity—there is no modernity without coloniality."

These scholars of decolonization and coloniality point out the subtleties of the insidious and ubiquitous nature of coloniality. According to them, coloniality has survived because its subtle nature allows it to be adopted by colonized subjects, without them realizing the extent to which they are participating in their own acculturation and oppression. In the words of Morgan Ndlovu (2018, 99), "coloniality manifests itself in terms of 'colonization of imagination,' 'colonization of the mind,' and colonization of knowledge and power."

Maldonado-Torres (2007, 243) describes it best when he states:

> Coloniality, instead, refers to a long-standing pattern of power that emerged as a result of colonialism, but that defines culture, labour, intersubjectivity relations, and knowledge production well beyond the strict limits of colonial administrations. Thus, coloniality survives colonialism. It is maintained alive in books, in the criteria for academic performance, in cultural patterns, in common sense, in the self-image of peoples, in aspirations of self, and so many other aspects of our modern experience. In a way, as modern subjects we breathe coloniality all the time and every day.

Scholars of modernity and coloniality (wa Thiong'o 1986, 2009; Maldonado-Torres 2006, 2007, 2011; Mignolo 2007, 2011; Murray-Miller, 2017; Ndlovu 2018; Ndlovu-Gatsheni 2019) argue that although most colonized countries have gained independence from former European colonial powers, they have yet to free their minds, their cultures, their indigenous epistemologies, and education systems. Most education systems and development programs are still based on externally oriented epistemologies.

Ndlovu-Gatsheni (2019) insists that colonialism profoundly impacted learning and identity issues in Africa, and as such, when the issues of epistemologies and mindset are solved, then and only then, can Africa start to strategize for development and growth. It is therefore imperative for decoloniality scholars to design a theoretical and praxis framework of decolonization as well as a pedagogical praxis that can serve as concept maps for future leadership, development, and social transformation in Africa. Ndlovu-Gatsheni (2019) concludes by saying that epistemic freedom can only happen when Africans put their phenomena at the center of any inquiry that involves them by beginning to see, think, and conceptualize the world from their own perspective and worldview instead of from the perspective of others. Thus, decoloniality questions the Eurocentric hegemony, which erases other ways of knowing, and it champions epistemic freedom and diversity. Consequently, decoloniality constitutes an enterprise that aims at creating a world where all forms of creating and transmitting knowledge are seen as equal and valid on a global level (Barongo-Muweke 2016).

In Africa the fight for independence and achieving political self-governance demonstrated that Africans could defeat the colonizers. Africans won without advanced war technologies. This boosted their self-esteem as opposed to the African Americans who live daily with the colonizers and slave masters within systemic racism. On a daily basis, the wound and collective trauma is reopened and dealt with in most cases at individual level with no institutional support.

When sub-Saharan African immigrants are confronted with racism and discrimination in the United States, at first their attitude is to dismiss it and assume that they can succeed despite all these challenges in their new environment. They believe because they are already familiar with and used to dealing with political and sociocultural challenges, they can cope with American racism and still thrive. Further, they believe that by being compliant and law abiding, they can earn respect and support to integrate into United States communities with little to no discrimination. The rhetoric that the United States has about equality, fairness, hard work ethics, and human rights tends to convince many sub-Saharan African immigrants who come to the United States searching for all these ideals, that they can succeed. Eventually they come to the realization that these ideals are myths and illusions. The concepts of democracy, equality, and humanity that the United States preaches around the world are not fully evident in this country given all the racism, police brutality against people of color, and discrimination based on gender and sexualities.

Many of our respondents have experienced instances of marginalization and exclusion firsthand. One respondent shares his experience as an outsider within as follows:

Being an immigrant is fun, challenging and it is interesting. Why I use those three words is because fun is you get exposed to too much, it is interesting because you get tried at every angle and you pick up things you have never seen, you meet many people and all that. It is challenging, in that there are many endless battles to fight, if your mind is not together you can give up. That is how I can sum that up.

Belonging requires a relational approach, which is not often felt by immigrants, as expressed by these two respondents:

It is knowing your place in this country, that you don't belong. It means working hard and trying to fit in.
As an immigrant, I feel guilty, but I appreciate all the opportunities that they have given us, economic opportunities but also opportunities to open up our minds. The problem with living just among us, living in Senegal, you don't question the values.

Some of our respondents expressed a feeling of alienation and being torn between two worlds and cultures as follows:

I think at the beginning when you immigrate, you are young, you are hopeful. You believe all societies are the same. You can live in the West, you can live back home in the traditional and modern settings. Then, with time and age and when you have children and they become socialized. You then realize first of all you don't belong anywhere anymore. You don't belong back home because your mentality has shifted, your way of life has shifted. You come here and you are still traditional enough that you don't belong here either, your way of thinking is completely different. So, I think the word that comes to mind is alienation, you feel alienated no matter where you are, you just don't belong anymore.

Many of our participants have reported that they have experienced linguistic profiling. As discussed in Chapter 3, the issue of accent can be a double-edged sword: On the one hand, it eases the interpersonal biases and discrimination (compliant and not threatening because of being continental African). But on the other hand, it does not save the sub-Saharan Africans from being targets of institutionalized racism and discrimination that comes from being Black in the United States. One of the respondents mirrored this in the following words:

Once I got to work it was hard not to notice that I was getting paid less because of gender and race. Another one expressed a similar experience when he stated that "In other places just being Black in America, you are Black doesn't matter whether you are from Africa or not." If you are from Africa, you worry about, especially before you get your papers, your immigration. You worry about all the things that could affect your chances of accomplishing the goals you want to in this country.

Discussing how nationality and accent are used to disqualify immigrants from jobs, one respondent recounts his experience in the following words:

I think my nationality has hindered me because before coming here I was already a professional in Nigeria. I was already working for an American company and I thought coming here was going to be easier for me to get a job. I really didn't know what I was going to expect, getting a job in my profession was not easy and I think part of it was because of my nationality and the way that I speak. I think I got turned down because of it, personally I think I did well in those interviews but I got turned down because of my name, they were not really sure if I could do the job or not.

Another respondent tells of a similar experience:

I applied to so many jobs and sometimes I never get a callback, so I do believe that it has to do with my nationality. Like as soon as I say my name that might be a red flag, accent and stuff. I just feel like that's a red flag in companies.

Racism has created a divide-and-conquer mentality between the oppressors and the oppressed. Audre Lorde (1984) invites us to see our differences as an asset that should bring to bear our commonalities, rather than exacerbate our differences. She explains that our differences should be seen as an embodiment of our diverse humanity and our interdependence, rather than as a source of division. In her words:

Institutional rejection of difference is an absolute necessity in a profit economy which needs outsiders as surplus people. As members of such an economy, we have all been programmed to respond to the human differences between us with fear and loathing and to handle that difference in one of three ways: ignore it, and if that is not possible, copy it if we think it is dominant, or destroy it if we think it is subordinate. But we have no patterns for relating across our human differences as equals. As a result, those differences have been misnamed and misused in the service of separation and confusion. (Lorde 1984, 115)

We tend to always see our differences as negative because it has always been a justification to discriminate against people. There is a distinctive reason why we refer to our differences as negatively impacting our unity instead of being unique and useful to humanity. Lorde (1984, 115) gives a good understanding as to how we see our differences as negative, "For we have all been raised in a society where these distortions were endemic within our living." There are many groups who have been victims of systemic oppression, for example, old people, people of color, people with disabilities, LBGTQ+, poor people and people with low-paying jobs. It is imperative that we engage in a paradigm shift in our understanding of differences in such a way that we do not automatically assume that those who are different from us are inferior, thus creating a separation between all people and preventing us from social change. According to Lorde, our ability to survive as a species in the future will depend on our ability to treat each other with dignity and respect on equal terms, rather than on an assumed biological hierarchy of the inferiority of some and the superiority of others. She underscores that idea when she affirms that, "Our future survival is predicated upon our ability to relate within equality" (Lorde 1984, 122).

As sub-Saharan African immigrants tell their stories and share the trials and tribulations they have endured in order to come to and survive in the United States, others may become not only more empathetic and appreciative of the insights that sub-Saharan African immigrants bring to the United States experience, but more understanding and respectful of the hard work ethics of immigrants in general. The prevalent perception in the West is that Africa is a continent of backward people who have no agency and no consciousness about their material conditions. The first European explorers who set foot on the African continent, as well as many who never did, approached Africa with their own preconceived biases about the African continent and its inhabitants, many of which have not changed. Thus, they deliberately distorted the reality to fit their perceptions of Africa and Africans. Such a mindset is what has allowed Hegel, the German philosopher who never set foot in Africa, to refer to it as the "dark continent." According to Hegel, Africa has nothing to offer humanity. In the same vein, John Locke, a London merchant who sailed to West Africa in 1561, referred to Africans as "beasts who have no houses," and the British poet, Rudyard Kipling referred to Africans as "half devil, half child" (Adichie 2009).

As discussed earlier, decoloniality as a tool for resisting colonialism has existed as long as colonialism. Resisting coloniality of power, coloniality of knowledge, coloniality of being, and decoloniality of the concept of "empty land or space" continues to date. Herodotus and many other Greek philosophers documented the depth and breadth of the knowledge that ancient Egyptians, who were Black, had. Herodotus and others acknowledged that the Greeks learned from Africans. They all wrote about and described how advanced Africans were. However, as Cheik Anta Diop and Theophile Obenga's research shows, the erasure and falsification of African history continues.

Narratives centered on White saviors and male heroes recorded history from a Eurocentric worldview and have led to the justification of the enslavement of Africans and the colonization of the African continent. This singularity has also been used to set world standards of intelligence, education, success, beauty, culture, language, and religion, including what constitutes worth and the definition of humanity. This is what Africans and African scholars resist when they use pedagogies of coloniality and demodernization.

When sub-Saharan African immigrants arrive in the United States, many try to assimilate to United States culture, and their mindset becomes influenced by those abovementioned stereotypes and perceptions that Westerners have of them. Many quickly realize that no matter what their sociocultural, economic, or political status, they are not immune to acts of racism. For example, this world has never been an easy place to dwell in for anyone who was less than whatever the current beauty structure and standards are. Some sub-Saharan African immigrants, due to pressure to assimilate, might resort to using cosmetic procedures, methods to lighten skin, make-up, and weight loss (that might lead to eating disorders such as anorexia or bulimia conditions) as discussed in Chapter 6, just to fit in or avoid the mean things that may be said if they are not compliant. So they do not challenge the status quo but adhere to mainstream standards of beauty.

In his research on African-Caribbean immigrants in the United States, (Johnson, 2019) found similar issues as the authors are discussing here. He states that African-Caribbean immigrants whom he interviewed described an experience of "sudden realization, or epiphany, about race in America. In addition to becoming aware of the different reality of race in America from the Caribbean, the participants described becoming aware that the American perspective on race subjected them to ill-treatment simply because they are Black" (Johnson, 2019, 67).

Similarly, our respondents have experienced these kinds of conflicts including the belief that to live in Europe is the definition of success, without recognizing that hardships also exist in Europe, and that if one returns to their native country poor, then they must "be a real idiot to come back" (Diome 2006, 58). Family members also place undue pressure on those who migrated to be successful, provide for their families, and they see them as "the family's social security" (Diome 2006, 27). This type of mental colonization is demonstrated in some of the responses of our participants:

What do I have to show back home? I would like to have a home there. Working in a predominantly White company my accent is made fun of, then I stand out since I am the only one in my department, my view point is sometimes ignored, then stereotypes that I have to debunk and being everyone's teacher about Africa and African students.

These participants' responses illustrate the pressure for financial support and untenable expectations that sub-Saharan African immigrants bear from their families and communities back home. The responses also underscore the dilemma of living in a very individualistic Western country while having to live by the collectivist/(communal) values and expectations of their African cultures. Other immigrants want to portray an unrealistic image of their lives in the West by either depicting only their successes and omitting their struggles, or by simply and deliberately choosing to mirror a life that is so utterly perfect that it has nothing to do with reality.

How do our participants navigate those contradictions, the pressures, and dealing with the polarities? While the sense of African collectivism guarantees support and solidarity for all members of a given group, many African immigrants isolate themselves in times when they need that societal support the most. Indeed, when African immigrants feel that they have failed to be successful and meet the expectations that either they or their families back home have set, they become overwhelmed with feelings of shame and guilt, and therefore fail to share with their families and communities the hardships that they are experiencing abroad. Some feel that they have brought shame to their families and that sharing the harsh details of their lived realities will be difficult for their families to hear and process.

References

Adichie, Chimamanda Ngozi. 2009. "The Danger of A Single Story." Ted Talk. October 7, 2009. YouTube video. www.youtube.com/watch?v=D9Ihs24lzeg.

Barongo-Muweke, Norah. 2016. *Decolonizing Education: Towards Reconstructing a Theory of Citizenship Education for Postcolonial Africa*. Wiesbaden: Springer.

Baum, Sandy and Stella M. Flores. 2011. "Higher Education and Children in Immigrant Families." *The Future of Children* 21, no. 1: 171–93. doi:10.1353/foc.2011.0000.

Crenshaw, Kimberle. 1989. "Demarginalizing the Intersection of Race and Sex: A Black Feminist Critique of Antidiscrimination Doctrine, Feminist Theory and Antiracist Politics." *University of Chicago Legal Forum* Vol. 1989, Article 8. https://chicagounbound.uchicago.edu/uclf/vol1989/iss1/8.

Davidson, Basil. 1994. *Modern Africa: A Social and Political History*. New York: Routledge.

Diome, Fatou. 2006. *The Belly of the Atlantic*. London: Serpent's Tail.

Fanon, Frantz. 1967. *Black Skin, White Masks*. New York: Grove Press

———. 1969. *The Wretched of the Earth*. London: Penguin.

Foucault, Michel. 1980. *Power/Knowledge: Selected Interviews and Other Writings 1972–77*, edited by Colin Gordon. New York: Pantheon Books.

Griffin, Kimberly A., Meghan J. Pifer, Jordan R. Humphrey and Ashley M. Hazelwood. 2011. "(Re)Defining Departure: Exploring Black Professors' Experiences with and Responses to Racism and Racial Climate." *American Journal of Education* 117, no. 4: 495–526.

Johnson, J. L., Bottorff, J. L., Browne, A. J., Grewal, S., Hilton, B. A. and Clarke, H. 2004. Othering and Being Othered in the Context of Health Care Services. *Health Communication* 16, no. 2: 255–71.

Johnson, R., 2019. *Negotiating American Racial Constructs: First-Generation African Caribbean Immigrants' Experience with Race*. Western Michigan University.

Kipling, R. and Wise, T. J. 1898. *The White Man's Burden*. London: McClure.

Kiramba, Lydiah Kananu, Adaurennaya C. Onyewuenyi, Alex Kumi-Yeboah, and Anthony Mawuli Sallar. 2020. "Navigating Multiple Worlds of Ghanaina-born Immigrant Adolescent Girls in US Urban Schools." *International Journal of Intercultural Relations* 77: 46–57.

Lirola, Maria Martinez. 2013. *Discourses on Immigration in Times of Economic Crisis*. Newcastle-upon-Tyne: Cambridge Scholars Publisher.

Lorde, Audre. 1984. *Sister Outsider Essays and Speeches*. New York: The Crossing Press.

———. 1995. "Age, Race, Class, and Sex: Women Redefining Differences." In *Words of Fire: An Anthology of African-American Feminist Thought*, edited by Beverly Guy-Sheftall, 284–91. New York: Seabury Press.

Maldonado-Torres, N. 2006. "Reconciliation as a Contested Future: Decolonization as Project or beyond the Paradigm of War. In *Reconciliation: Nations and Churches in Latin America*, edited by Iain S. Maclean, 225–45. Alder shot, England: Ashgate.

Maldonado-Torres, Nelson. 2007. "On the Coloniality of Being: Contributions to the Development of a Concept 1." *Cultural Studies* 21, no. 2–3: 243.

Maldonado-Torres, N. 2011. Thinking through the Decolonial Turn: Post-Continental Interventions in Theory, Philosophy, and Critique—An Introduction. *TRANSMODERNITY: Journal of Peripheral Cultural Production of the Luso-Hispanic World* 1, no. 2.

Maundeni, T. 1999. "African Females and Adjustment to Studying Abroad." *Gender and Education* 11, no. 1: 27–42.

Mignolo, W. D. 2007. "Delinking: The Rhetoric of Modernity, the Logic of Coloniality and the Grammar of De-coloniality. *Cultural Studies* 21, nos. 2 and 3: 449–514.

Mignolo, Walter D. 2011. *The Darker Side of Western Modernity: Global Futures, Decolonial Options*. Durham, NC: Duke University Press.

Moran, Mark. 2021. "APA Board Issues Apology for History of Racism." *Psychiatric News* 56, 2. https://doi.org/10.1176/appi.pn.2021.2.45.

Murray-Miller, Gavin. 2017. *The Cult of the Modern: Trans-Mediterranean France and the Construction of French Modernity*. Lincoln: University of Nebraska Press.

Ndlovu, Morgan. 2018. "Coloniality of Knowledge and the Challenge of Creating African Futures." *Ufahamu: A Journal of African Studies* 40, no. 2. https://doi.org/10.5070/F7402040944.

Ndlovu-Gatsheni, Sabelo J. 2019. "Discourses of Decolonization/Decoloniality." *Papers on Language & Literature* 55, no. 3: 201–300.

———. 2021. "Decolonization in the 21st Century: Sabelo Ndlovu-Gatsheni in Conversation with Eman Shaban Morsi." Dartmouth University. May 20, 2021. YouTube video. www.youtube.com/watch?v=6szwPsCq_f4.

Ngugi wa Thiong'o. 1986. *Decolonizing the Mind: The Politics of Language in African Literature.* London: James Currey.

Ngugi wa Thiong'o. 2009. *Re-Membering Africa.* Nairobi/Kampala/Dar es Salaam: East African Educational Publishers Ltd.

Okeke-Ihejirika, Philomina, Gillian Creese, Michael Frishkopf, and Njoki Wane. 2020. "Re-envisioning Resilience from African Immigrants' Perspectives." *Canadian Ethnic Studies* 52, no. 3: 129–49. https://doi.org/10.1353/ces.2020.0030.

Oliphant, Sarah Moore. 2019. "Voices of Ethiopian Immigrant Women." *International Social Work* 62, no. 2: 581–94.

Patricia Hill Collins. 2000. *Black Feminist Thought: Knowledge, Consciousness, and the Politics of Empowerment.* New York: Routledge.

Shizha, Edward, Ali A. Abdi, Stacey Wilson-Forsberg, and Oliver Masakure. 2020. "African Immigrant Students and Postsecondary Education in Canada: High School Teachers and School Career Counsellors as Gatekeepers." *Canadian Ethnic Studies* 52, no. 3: 67–86.

Thomas, Kevin J. A. and Ikubolajeh Logan. 2012. "African Female Immigration to the United States and Its Policy Implications." *Canadian Journal of African Studies/La Revue canadienne des études africaines* 46, no. 1: 87–107.

Thornton, Bonnie Dill and Zambrane. 2009. "Critical Thinking about Inequality: An Emerging Lens." In *Feminist Theory Reader: Local and Global Perspectives,* 176–86. New York, NY: Routledge.

Walsh, Catherine E. 2018. "The Decolonial For: Resurgences, Shifts, and Movements." In *On Decoloniality: Concepts, Analytics, Praxis,* edited by Walter D. Mignolo and Catherine E. Walsh, 15–32. Durham, NC: Duke University Press.

Waters, Mary C. 2014. "Defining Difference: The Role of Immigrant Generation and Race in American and British Immigration Studies." *Ethnic and Racial Studies* 37, no. 1: 10–26.

Chapter 6

COPING STRATEGIES AS WE RECLAIM
OUR IDENTITY AND VOICES
OF POWER

*In this merging he wishes neither of the older selves to be lost. He would not Africanize
America, for America has too much to teach the world and Africa. He would
not bleach his Negro soul in a flood of white Americanism, for he knows that Negro
blood has a message for the world. He simply wishes to make it possible for a man
to be both a Negro and an American, without being cursed and spit upon by his
fellows, without having the doors of opportunity closed roughly in his face.*
                              —W. E. B. Du Bois, *The Souls of Black Folk*

Conscious Dissemblance

*Me and my captain don't agree
But he don't know, 'cause he don't ask me
He don't know he don't know my mind
When he sees me laughing
Laughing to keep from crying
Got one mind for white folk to see
Another for what I know is me.*

                                        —Unknown Laborer

In this chapter, the authors expound on how sub-Saharan African
immigrants deal with and recreate new transnational identities by discussing
some trends of behavior that seem to be used to deal with critical identity
issues. Here the authors explore a variety of strategies—from assimilation,
integration, and compromising to adapting and reevaluating their ways of
thinking and behaving to the American context—adopted by sub-Saharan

African immigrants for coping with racism and discrimination based on skin color, language, specifically accent, the transnational dimension of place of origin and other intersecting identities. This chapter also deals with the difficult reality of the lack of validation that many immigrants feel in the United States.

As sub-Saharan African immigrants, we come with our own understanding and definition of success, and we also bring our communities' and families hopes and aspirations for success. We do everything that America says one needs to do to succeed, but there are so many impediments and outside forces to that success. To fit in and become as American as we can, we go to such extremes, including bleaching our skins and straightening our hair. And yet even that is not enough. We also come possessing a high level of self-esteem and confidence in our cultures and values demonstrated in our fashion and food. However, this does not last long. The stares and glares in the hallways, elevators and streets, and comments loaded with covert racism eventually cause some sub-Saharan Africans to abandon their beautiful fashions and adopt a "blue jeans and T-shirt" culture. Instead of healthy home-cooked meals, they drift toward the mac and cheese and burger lifestyle just to fit in. They work hard at Americanizing their English too. Only the very brave retain a bit of their culture, fashion and participation in advocacy through civic and campus events and the occasional (if any) African night celebrations found in some institutions of higher education and local communities during Black History Month.

As immigrants from sub-Saharan Africa, as soon as we open our mouths to speak, we are almost always asked the question, "You have an accent, where are you from?" Sometimes this loaded question implies that we are foreigners and not Americans because of our accent. From there, depending on the person who is asking the question, the conversation could go in any direction, ranging from simple curiosity to overt or covert racism. The question itself, innocent or not, places issues of identity and place of origin into the foreground of the conversation and directs the participants' responses.

There are other Americans who treat sub-Saharan African immigrants as immature and needing guidance and support. However, after a few more interactions, when these same Americans realize that sub-Saharan African immigrants are well equipped to navigate their environment, their stance changes, and they start to blame those around the immigrants for changing them into troublemakers. The reason why Americans first viewed sub-Saharan African immigrants as "safe" was their definition of who is threatening and who is not. Sub-Saharan African immigrants come off as innocent, curious, safe and less threatening because they are compared to

African Americans who are always labeled as loud and angry regardless of whether or not they fit that mold. These labels have become institutionalized wedges that racists use to divide Black people, whether they are from the continent, the islands, or the United States.

Once they are in the country, other challenges emerge including food and culture, parenting, family and its dynamics, health care, housing, recreation, engaging in community and civic activities, reconciling conflicting values and beliefs, isolation and social support, financial pressures to support self and continue to support family back in their country of origin, United States politics, credit score systems, and the filing of taxes. Other challenges include academic success, personal development, job performance, and motivation to succeed.

This is well illustrated by the following comment from one of our respondents:

Definitely it is a different culture, you have to learn, you have to adapt and you cannot live like you are in Africa.

Another shared the same sentiment when he says:

As a man you have to adapt and put up with the change. Major values we have had to compromise, adapt and re-evaluate: Sharing house work since here we can't afford house help, becoming more independent, working different shifts with my wife, improved communication.

Another challenge of adapting was expressed by another respondent who claimed that:

Kitchen rules also had to change. I had to adapt and learn to do kitchen chores. Even when baby was born, I also had to adapt to being close to my baby, which is not expected, and yet I am enjoying time with my baby and the bonding. Accommodating both cultures and adapting has been interesting and a learning experience.

Other identity issues include the use of hair extensions, straightening of hair, and the phenomenon of skin bleaching, as well as translanguaging and code switching as strategies of coping and fitting in. Voluntary depigmentation is a direct result of the imposition and globalization of Whiteness, which is a symbol of the internalization of Western beauty standards. The motivations for using skin-bleaching products might be diverse, but the aim remains the same for almost all those who bleach their skin: the desire to lighten their skin color so that they can be perceived to be as white as possible, to help them improve their social standing. In order to achieve this aim, Africans who engage in this practice use a multitude of lightening products, most of the time with negative health consequences.

The data resulting from several studies conducted by dermatologists (Africans and non-Africans alike) on skin bleaching point to this problem as a primarily urban phenomenon. Many advertisements about skin depigmenting products tap into the aesthetic insecurities of dark-skinned Black women by carrying a message of a universal condemnation of Blackness. In the words of Arogundade (2000, 156), these black cosmetics are based on "ethnicity-altering" depigmenting products designed to rid the bodies of people of color of its "pathological" darkness. They continue to exploit the idea of the aesthetic inferiority of Black skin and the supremacy of Whiteness to promote their products. The manufacturers of these bleaching cosmetics and the media that promote them continue to make a fortune from the insecurity and complex of Black people. This cosmetic industry was worth $8.6 billion in 2020.

Ronald Hall (2006) blames the spreading of voluntary depigmentation among people of color on Western cultural imperialism and oppression. According to him, there are two colonial factors that are responsible for the internalization of Western beauty ideals by women of color. The first one is the elevation of Whiteness as the essence of feminine beauty, and the second one is the subsequent invasion of African markets by Western cosmetic products that promise a lighter skin in a tube (Hall 2006, 31).

Tackling the issue of the invasion of Africa by Western aesthetic values transmitted through the media, Marita Golden (2004, 151) affirms the following:

> The invasion of European and American films and television programs, with their exaltation of White female beauty, White male heroism, White economic and social power, White life, and, by extension White skin, are only part of the problem. Mass media is an intoxicating drug, a potent form of propaganda. But this ongoing cultural narrative has interacted with African minds poisoned by generations of "psychological colonialism" and shame among some at many things African.

There is a tendency on the part of many Africans to assimilate to Western life and for many, that means trying as much as possible to be closer to Whiteness by getting rid of their Africaness as a cultural reference point. On a deeper level, artificial depigmentation is the outward manifestation of cultural oppression.

The issue is really a cultural one in the sense that it translates Africans' unwillingness to assume their cultural identity. By succumbing to Western beauty ideals as their reference point, the psychology of the excessive desire for lighter skin at all costs embodies the perception that those who artificially lighten their skin consciously or subconsciously want to emulate Whiteness.

Indeed, the desire and fascination that Africans have with the White man's skin and its internalization as the ultimate aesthetic ideal, despite the health risks that such a practice entails, cannot but denote the fact that Western standards of beauty have overtaken African ones. Many Africans associate Whiteness with beauty and cleanliness. On a psychological level, voluntary depigmentation constitutes one element of the commercialization of Whiteness on a global level. It also translates the internal struggle for identity that Africans are waging. It plays the role of a mask that allows those who put it on to hide their discomfort "vis-à-vis" their Black skin. (Konaté 2009)

Some of the coping mechanisms adopted by sub-Saharan African immigrants can take different such as from assimilating, compromising, adapting and reevaluating their ways of thinking and behaving to the American context (as was evident in the responses discussed earlier); coming to the realization that there is need to change styles and structures of communication with others; dealing with new pressures on intimate relationships; the constant emotional and cognitive strain brought about by the new realities of relocation; and the need to be grounded in African cultures and to maintain their African identity. The following respondents underscore this message:

> When you come here because you are able to sustain yourself and do all kinds of things. Then this country makes you shift all kinds of things and that puts a huge strain and I don't know if it is for all African men but for most African men when there is that shift it just changes everything.
>
> Coming from Africa you have an extended family where your aunt and nieces help you. Here, you don't have any help so I just realized very quickly if she doesn't get help she is going to burn out; if she burns out I am going to lose so I had to learn. First, I had to read books about different subjects. I had to read books because I didn't see it growing up.
>
> Different values, cultures, and expectations. I grew up in a rural town and coming to America was so different. We did not forget where we are from. We have always maintained that we are from Africa and this is what we need to do. We kind of incorporate the American culture into the best part of it and also brought our African heritage and culture into it.

Sub-Saharan African immigrants who are raising children devise coping strategies to include children's well-being, safety, education, acculturation, and assimilation. Most parents fear that their children will be lost if they are not anchored in their African values and are concerned that they will get involved in illegal or immoral activities as they assimilate to American culture. The way housing is designed in the United States is different from Africa. Most immigrants select places where there are other immigrants or places where they can afford, and these tend to be inner city housing designed for low-income people. Inadvertently, it also turns out to be some of the places where crime rates are higher.

One respondent captures the cultural shift that most sub-Saharan African immigrants have to make:

> Yes, some expectations back home are not imposed on me here. My husband can help me with the baby and house chores without feeling the pressure of being expected to be a "man." For young girls it can be too much freedom unlike back home where men are freer especially in issues of relationships.

One respondent expressed the importance of striking a balance between the cultures as a coping strategy:

> In Africa, we couldn't bring the whole culture here, we brought the best parts of the ones here and said hey we gotta do it, we gotta make it work somehow. So we made it work and it has been a great journey so far.

Having to constantly confront these challenges has caused sub-Saharan African immigrants to learn to operate in both worlds as much as it causes emotional fatigue and a huge financial burden. Sub-Saharan African immigrants are working and living in foreign adopted countries and yet supporting families back in their native land as discussed in Chapter 4. They also have to participate socially by contributing to baby showers, weddings and funerals. In these days of social media, they attend via Zoom and WhatsApp, family meetings and get involved in family conflict resolutions and daily social functions that are important for maintaining the social fabric.

One other respondent shares how they have adapted and reevaluated their ways of thinking and behaving to the American context:

> I am married to a Nigerian like myself, so we still hold on to Nigerian cultural values. Although we come from two different ethnic groups, there are general cultural belief systems that run through different

ethnic groups in my country. Even if you married an African from say Liberia or Ghana or Sierra Leone or Kenya there are certain cultural traits that run through many African countries so that does not have necessarily have relative impact.

Dealing with new pressures on family relationships and the constant emotional and cognitive strain brought about by the new realities of relocation, one respondent states:

> I think that because here work is demanding you have to be smart and think about it. Since I travelled a lot, I took my family everywhere I could take them before the kids started going to school. So, I think family is very important to me, to bring them with me as much as possible because I do not want to succeed professionally and lose my family.

Research methodologies are also problematic in that most of them are quantitative, following the bell curve, and as such, data from the outlier is never taken seriously, as it is regarded as not representative of the population. Yet most minoritized groups are usually outliers unless they are the focus of the study. Minoritized scholars researching on issues affecting their groups are always labeled troublemakers, especially because of the stereotypes that view them as docile and require them to play nicely in the sandbox. They are further viewed as very peaceful, conciliatory and non-threatening. The moment they start speaking truth to power, they are seen as disruptive and troublemakers. For these authors, finding literature that incorporated the lived experiences of sub-Saharan African immigrants and their stories was challenging.

As continental African women who live in the West, we continue to hold the position of outsiders within. An added position is that of being the bridge between two worlds. We live in the United States, but at the same time, we bear the same responsibilities vis-á-vis our families back home as if we were still living there. We are expected to take care of our parents and immediate families financially and emotionally, in addition to all the other social responsibilities that women are traditionally expected to fulfill in African societies. These include raising families, attending family and community functions, such as weddings, naming ceremonies and funerals, and providing moral support to family members, friends and neighbors who need it.

In the West, the racial dynamics converge with the gender ones to further marginalize us. For example, we often get this feeling that our White colleagues in the United States do not take us seriously. They also do not think that we are smart enough to understand the subtleties of the racial and gender dynamics in the United States. More importantly, we are not even seen as being able to think for ourselves to be able to analyze a situation and form our own opinion about it. The moment we speak up or disagree, we become a problem. However, we have chosen to be what they call us—troublemakers. Like John Lewis would say, if you want to get into trouble, choose "good trouble," "necessary trouble."

We are disruptors and troublemakers in multiple ways because we have chosen to remove ourselves from our societies and countries by emigrating to the West. We have also made a conscious choice not to pass on oppressive aspects of our native cultures to our children, thus breaking the chain of dysfunction and refusing to be the vectors of transmission of cultural practices that are detrimental to us, as well as to our children and their future progenitors. Moreover, we have chosen not to be silent participants in cultures that have silenced and oppressed us, by speaking up and writing about their detrimental aspects.

Furthermore, we are disruptors because we have chosen to be bridges between our cultures of origin and our adoptive cultures. We have done so by synthesizing and retaining the positive aspects of both, as well as creating a new culture and way of life that makes sense to us, that affirms us, values us, humanizes us, and celebrates us by acknowledging our importance and contributions to our families, our communities, and this world in general. Deonne Minto (2007, 1, 7) argues, "Black women writers use their literary works to unsettle the dominant gendered racial hierarchy, to critique national discourses, and to offer a vision of a transnational America." This is in no doubt the case for the authors of this book who live in two worlds much as do their respondents.

It is for these reasons that we embarked on a journey of telling our own stories to demonstrate that the power we have is actually our voice. We also realized in the process of researching this book that we have more power than we are allowed and that causes many anti-immigrant sentiments.

Researchers' Reflection: Fredah Mainah, PhD

My parents were born and grew up in a colonial rule environment, as did their parents. They could not even dare to attempt to define themselves as freedom fighters, let alone get involved in such activities or else they would have found themselves imprisoned as dissidents or dead as terrorists. I believe they knew how empowering it was possessing personal agency, determination and freedom of choice, and that is why they fought the colonial powers. You cannot miss that which you did not know. My ancestors knew freedom and integrity and thus the freedom-fighting history.

The achievement of independence by former European colonies forced them to quickly assimilate their colonial masters' culture and firmly entrenched idea that a nation should have male-dominated leadership. Women's histories, wisdom and ways of knowing, their issues, and sociocultural and socioeconomic involvement were made secondary or completely excluded.

I was lucky in that my parents did not strictly adhere to those norms, and so chores at home or on the farm were allocated by age, not gender. They also allowed their daughters to get an education in whatever area they chose from the available careers. I started teaching at 18 before attending college. Although I wished to become a journalist, that was not available for women at the time.

I came to the United States via the Diversity Visa lottery generally referred to as the Green Card. Equipped with a British-oriented education and knowledge of the English language, I believed I could get a job immediately and without a lot of challenges. However, the reality was different. Many recruiters did not understand this visa category nor did they spare me discrimination because of my accent. To cope, I decided to go back to college to get another master's degree that I hoped would be easily recognizable by the recruiters. Indeed, it worked.

However, it left me perturbed and with many unanswered questions. Choosing to take on American citizenship almost means losing any other we hold. If one comes from a country that does not offer dual citizenship, then one by default has lost their native citizenship. What does it even mean to have dual citizenship when the country of origin is visited during vacations that do not last more than 30 days because of the nature of the jobs we hold in our foreign and adopted countries?

How do I continue from here where in a minute I am renouncing what I have been and now become this new American? How do I navigate that space and the emotions that go with it?

What did I just do by taking this new citizenship and renouncing my native one? How does an oath and a signature completely erase who I have been and usher me into being an American? Are my tears genuine? I left my native country to come to the United States for better opportunities, so why am I feeling like I am betraying my native land? Will I ever be American enough, given my color and accent? How will I now respond to those microaggressions and the questions of how can I be an American employee with that accent, and how long have you been in America that they gave you a job before you had "learned English"?

What am I now? What does my identity mean? Does my patriotism in my adopted country really count toward my identity in terms of those who are Americans by birth and those of us who are by citizenship, and therefore hold accepted political ideals, language, religion, culture, and so on?

Is it even possible to merge our multiple dimensions of identity given their diverse and fluid backgrounds? When I am visiting my native country, what is my identity? On my way back, at the airport, as I line up for security clearance, am I leaving behind one identity and assuming another, or am I at that time merging them? Are they propelling me to a world of identity conflict or to one of self-acceptance? When I go on vacation to my native country, the assumption of wealth is also placed on me, and I am expected to be more generous because I am "White" and rich. I am the savior and problem solver. My brother has even taken on debt because he tells his creditors that he has a sister abroad who will send him money soon.

It was my second year in the United States and my first back to college. I was a graduate research assistant at one of the local public universities that was predominantly White. My clothes were still what I had brought from Africa, which were mostly African-wear fashion and styles made from colorful and printed fabric. My hair was kinky combed into a short Afro. Most hallway and elevator contact was with curious Americans who wanted to know why I was wearing a costume in the summer. (I did not yet know about Halloween.) My attempt to explain that I was not in costume was not well understood. Those who were curious but not courageous enough to talk to me gave me stares that really made me uncomfortable. The days I wore jeans, they would be a size or two larger to cover my curves and not show them off, as my culture expected. I thought I was fitting in, but even that still attracted stares.

Eventually I used hair-softening chemicals to straighten my kinks. This attracted comments such as, " I didn't realize you had such long and good hair." I did not know what to make of such comments, and oftentimes I was too offended to speak. I also acquired a few fitting pairs of jeans in different color shades. I was making so much effort to fit in, yet the comments and stares would not stop. In the break room, the focus turned to my food and accent.

One day, I decided to end it all: I trimmed my hair short, trashed all my bottles of nail polish and pulled out my African wear. I was going to be my authentic self, and I was going to ignore all the stares and comments. And there began my brave journey to becoming an authentic African who is also American.

Researchers' Reflection: Mariam Konaté, PhD

As a continental African woman who grew up in a deeply patriarchal society with strictly enforced gender roles, I started to notice at a very young age the gender biases that were embedded in my culture. As the oldest of four children on my father's side, I quickly realized that although seniority comes with some perks, as a woman, I was not getting those seniority perks. In my culture, young women are groomed at a very tender age to learn how to cook and clean so that they can grow up to be good wives and mothers. We are told that acquiring an education will not be a buffer against having to learn how to cook and clean.

On the other hand, my younger brothers never had to cook, clean, or hand-wash their own clothes. As a woman, I had to hand-wash everyone's clothes, even my father's cloth handkerchief he uses to blow his nose with when he has a cold (no Kleenex then). I knew about my culture's gender biases toward women as I witnessed my own mother having to be the one to cook and clean and do all domestic related work. I also knew about the gender disparities through other forms of socialization that teach women that they should know their place in the patriarchal hierarchy. Indeed, women are told that their male partners have the right to lay their hand on them and that they are supposed to be seen and not heard. For example, when I got married, I was told that when my husband says, "One," I should not say, "Two," which implied that the man always has the first and last say, whether the woman agrees or not.

Most of us grew up in societies where we were silenced and not allowed to have either a voice or an opinion. Speaking up or even having an opinion was mostly met with corporal punishment. In my culture, when you spoke back or argued with an adult, you got a smack on the mouth with the back of the hand. We were expected to endure in silence. Married women and mothers are taught that patience and martyrdom eventually paid off. Mothers are told that if they endure and suffer in silence, their children will be successful in life. Buchi Emecheta captures that reality as expressed through Nnu Ego's predicament as a senior wife and mother in her novel *Joys of Motherhood*:

> Nnu Ego has allowed herself to wonder where it was she had gone wrong. She had been brought up to believe that children made a woman. She had had children, nine in all, and luckily, seven are alive, much more than many women of that period could boast of. [...] Still, how was she to know that by the time her children grew up the values of her country, her people and her tribe would have changed so drastically,

to the extent where a woman with many children could face a lonely
old age, and maybe a miserable death alone, just like a barren woman?
(Emecheta 1979, 219)

Moreover, I grew up noticing that as the beacons of the traditions, women
tend to participate in their own victimization. Women are the gatekeepers of
traditions. As such, they pass on those traditions to their daughters, even when
they are oppressive to them. For example, female genital cutting is a woman's
affair. Women are the ones who do it to other women, although it benefits men.
Mothers teach their daughters the cultural expectations and behaviors that end
up oppressing them as second-class citizens. The following conversation
between Nnu Ego and her co-wife, Adaku, underscores the ways in which
women become the handmaidens for patriarchy: "Maybe you are right again,
my senior. Yet the more I think about it the more I realize that we women
set impossible standards for ourselves. That we make life intolerable for one
another" (Emecheta 1979, 169). In that sense, women are outsiders within their
own cultures. Women live in cultures that literally treat them as less than.
As a result of their positionality in their own cultures, women are better placed
to critique those cultures from the standpoint as outsiders within (Lorde, 1984).

Most literature reviewed found that immigrants' coping effectiveness
reduced over time as a result of the burden of racism and discrimination
as well as the emotional toll from navigating the complex, diverse and
often contradicting American cultures and values. Rommel Johnson (2019)
expressed this concern in his research on Black Caribbeans who live
in the United States in contrast to those who come for a brief period of time
and leave. Johnson had lived in the United States for over 20 years by the time
of his publication. He shares his own pre- and post-immigration story, which
included his arrival, navigating multiple worlds, languages and cultures,
strategies of coping, assimilation, his lived experiences in the United States,
and eventually how racism and discrimination affected him and caused
his coping strategies to lose effectiveness over time:

While it (race) can include phenotypic features, such as skin color, hair
structure (straight, kinky/curly), and aspects of colorism are practiced,
it is much broader and includes education, family background, religion,
and profession. Before I moved to America, I had never thought much
about being Black or given attention to my skin tone's social implications.
I came to realize that, as a "light-skinned" Black person, I had privilege
in Dominica simply because my skin was considered light only when
I explored the way race is understood in the Caribbean [...]. I had
been in America for two years [...]. Disheartening thoughts came to

my mind as I realized slowly that, after making many sacrifices, I came to America to have a better life, yet my determination and intentions to work hard did not matter to a large segment of American society because I have black skin. I felt dehumanized. For several days after my epiphany about race in America, I recall generally feeling betrayed, frustrated, depressed, angry, and anxious. Processing this realization of race as it exists in American society was difficult because it created a huge dissonance. (Johnson 2019, 47, 49)

Most sub-Saharan African immigrants adopt constructive coping strategies by focusing on addressing the challenges they are facing. They constantly remind themselves of the expectations and goals they set or family set for them before entry. In order to deal with the multifaceted challenges that they face in the United States, a more holistic and multipronged approach would be an important step toward developing more effective models of studying coping strategies adopted by immigrants rather than focusing on only one dimension, such as the impact of racism. Immigrants often devise coping mechanisms that can be studied further and used to inform policy and programs (Yakushko 2010; Oriji 2019). Policymakers, educational administrators and civic leaders would be assisted by such models to design more effective strategies for making it easier for sub-Saharan African immigrants to settle and integrate in the United States.

References

Adichie, Chimamanda Ngozi. 2009. "The Danger of A Single Story." Ted Talk. October 7, 2009. YouTube video. www.youtube.com/watch?v=D9Ihs241zeg.

Arogundade, Ben. 2000. *Black Beauty: History and A Celebration.* London: Pavilion Books LTD.

Du Bois, W. E. B. 1953. *The Souls of Back Folk.* New York: Bantam Books.

Emecheta, Buchi. 1979. *The Joys of Motherhood.* New York: George Braziller.

Golden, Marita. 2004. *Don't Play in the Sun: One Woman's Journey Through the Color Complex.* New York: Doubleday.

Hall, Ronald E. 2006. *Bleaching Beauty: Light Skin as a Filipina Ideal.* Quezon City, Philippines: Giraffe Books.

Hobson, Janell. 2016. *Are All the Women Still White?* SUNY Series in Feminist Criticism and Theory. Albany: State University of New York Press.

Johnson, Rommel. 2019. "Negotiating American Racial Constructs: First-Generation African Caribbean Immigrants' Experience with Race." PhD dissertation Western Michigan University.

Konaté, Mariam. 2009. "Wearing a Mask: 'Voluntary De-pigmentation' among Continental Africans: An Aesthetic Revolution or a Post-Colonial Traumatism?" *Lagos Notes and Records* 15: 87–117.

Lorde, Audre. 1984. *Sister Outsider Essays and Speeches.* New York: The Crossing Press.

———. 1995. "Age, Race, Class, and Sex: Women Redefining Differences." In *Words of Fire:An Anthology of African-American Feminist Thought,* edited by Beverly Guy-Sheftall, 284–91. New York: Seabury Press.

Minto, Deonne. 2006. "Breaking through the Silence: Knowledge, the 'Racial Contract' and the 'Colonial Unconscious' in Cola Debrot's *My Sister the Negro*." *Dutch Crossing* 30, no. 1: 75–84, https://doi.org/10.1080/03096564.2006.11730872

———. 2007. "Sisters in the Spirit: Transnational Constructions of Diaspora in Late Twentieth-century Black Women's Literature of the Americas." PhD dissertation University of Maryland, College Park.

Offiah, Chivuzo and Silk Ogbu. 2017. "Understanding the Effects of the Media's Promotion of the 'Perfect Body' Image among Adolescent Girls in Lagos Nigeria." *Specialty Journal of Humanities and Cultural Science* 2, no. 3: 47–59.

Okeke-Ihejirika, Philomina. 2020. "Beyond Blackness: Sub-Saharan African Immigrant Knowledges and Agency in Canada." *Canadian Ethnic Studies* 52, no. 3: 1–5.

Okeke-Ihejirika, Philomina, Gillian Creese, Michael Frishkopf and Njoki Wane. 2020. "Re-envisioning Resilience from African Immigrants' Perspectives." *Canadian Ethnic Studies* 52, no. 3: 129–49.

Oriji, Chinwe Ezinna. 2019. "From Biafra to Police Brutality: Challenging Localized Blackness toward Globally Racialized Ethnicities of Nigerians in the U.S." *Ethnic and Racial Studies* 43, no. 9: 1600–17, https://doi.org/10.1080/01419870.2019.1649441.

Staples, Robert. 1970. "The Myth of the Black Matriarchy." *The Black Scholar* 1, nos. 3/4: 8–16.

Yakushko, Oksana. 2010. "Stress and Coping Strategies in the Lives of Recent Immigrants: A Grounded Theory Model." *International Journal for the Advancement of Counselling* 32, no. 4: 256–73. https://doi.org/10.1007/s10447-010-9105-1.

Chapter 7

THE MYTH OF GOING BACK HOME WHILE LIVING IN TWO WORLDS

Living with two hearts: "I'm Here but I'm There."

—W. E. B. Du Bois

In Chapter 7, the authors discuss the dilemma faced by sub-Saharan African immigrants trapped in the paradox and myth of going back to their native countries after graduation or "making it." While other researchers on African immigration suggest that the major reasons for immigration are economic or conflict-related, most of the respondents interviewed gave education and family reunification as their primary reasons for immigrating. Furthermore, the myth of going back home shows that the pursuit of education was to position them for better job opportunities back in their native countries. The researchers reflect on the myth held by many immigrants in the United States: the hope of one day going back home after completing education or getting the needed resources:

> You then realize first that you don't belong anywhere anymore. You don't belong back home because your mentality has shifted, your way of life has shifted. You come here and you are still traditional enough that you don't belong here either, your way of thinking is completely different. So, I think the word that comes to mind is alienation, you feel alienated no matter where you are, you just don't belong anymore. (Respondent)

The reason why most researchers of sub-Saharan African immigrants describe the hope of returning to their countries of origin as a myth is because as time passes, it becomes more of a mirage than a reality for most of them. They get caught between multiple worlds that have conflicting expectations of them. Their coping strategies lose effectiveness over time, and they soon realize that succeeding within the duration they had set for themselves or that was embedded in the college program they had chosen is not realistic.

Eventually, they adjust and decide to juggle school with economic pursuits just to survive. Some keep the "hope of return" by visiting their countries of origin as often as they can. The realization that they cannot fully return causes a dissonance while at the same time, it keeps their hopes up. They reason that they can at least earn a living in the United States and support their families back home, however limited that support is.

Most studies that deal with the theme of return to the home countries (Anwar 1979; Al-Rasheed 1994; Zetter 1999; King 2000; Ammassari and Black 2001), rarely discuss the intentions about returning home permanently that most immigrants have when they first emigrate (Mensah 2010). Most of the participants, including the authors, emigrated for specific reasons, and planned to return home once those aims were achieved. The intention of returning home takes the form of a "myth," as in an unachievable and unfulfilled desire for many diaspora and refugee populations who, for either political or historical reasons and circumstances, cannot fulfill their dream of physically returning to their countries of origin (Anwar 1979; Al-Rasheed 1994; Zetter 1999). For all other immigrant groups, however, "Continually delayed, permanent return acquires the status of a myth" (Mensah 2010, 153).

As a researcher-participant, and one of the co-authors of this book (Konaté), I left my home country of Burkina Faso in the winter of 1994 not only to join my then-husband but to also pursue graduate studies. Before I left, we had discussed our intention to get our respective graduate degrees and return to pursue successful careers in our home country. However, my plans to return home were derailed by the realities of a prolonged graduate degree trajectory while raising a family. By the time I graduated in 2004, I no longer met the maximum age requirement for qualifying for a government job position in my country, and at that time, I had far better employment opportunities and a more promising future raising my young family in the United States than returning home. Burkina Faso has an age limit of 30 years for government hiring, and by the time I graduated, I was over this required age limit. I also realized that I could help my parents and other family members back home more by staying and working in the United States than if I were to go back. In other words, I came to the realization that I had more chances of achieving an improved financial position to help my family back home by staying permanently in the United States and visiting them in Burkina Faso periodically. So, I chose to stay in the United States.

In his research about sub-Saharan African immigrants in Canada, Mensah (2010) describes the internal dilemma that sub-Saharan African immigrants experience between their initial decision to return home and the more pressing reality of staying in the host country. According to him, this ambivalence between going back home and staying in the host country is caused by the pressures that immigrants feel to integrate into their host countries, and "is more perceptible in international migration because of the greater physical and sociocultural distance, larger cost, and the greater psychic burden and apprehension that are inherent in decisions to migrate on an international scale" (Mensah 2010, 110–11). He goes on to say "the manifestations of this mismatch are not hard to see among international migrants, especially those travelling a longer distance to a relatively different cultural milieu such as Sub-Saharan Africans migrating to Canada" (Mensah 2010, 110–11).

In Fatou Diome's novel titled *The Belly of the Atlantic* (2006), the main character, Salie, decides to move away from Senegal and create a life for herself in France. She wants to begin studying to be a writer, but that idea quickly goes downhill when the reality of her life sets in. She still feels tied to home through her brother whose only concern is football. He wants to run away to France to become successful, but Salie doesn't have the heart to tell him that there is no golden country where all your aspirations can be fulfilled. Senegal is a society like other African nations that prides itself on the successes of their loved ones. *The Belly of the Atlantic* gives a glimpse of the familial pressures to support their loved ones left behind in Senegal when people migrate to another country, like France. "After the historically recognized colonization, a kind of mental colonization now prevails," and "everything desirable comes from France" (Diome, 2006, 32).

Salie often compares the individualistic community where she lives to her past life in Senegal. Even though she makes a path for herself, she seems to question her decision frequently. She tries to spread the message that each country has false expectations of the other, and they are uninformed when it comes to what happens there. She doesn't feel at home in France or in Senegal. The ability to obtain material items and provide monetary support are tangible signs of accomplishments. Salie doesn't have the courage to tell her brother that there is no golden country where all one's aspirations can be fulfilled. Salie describes how her dreams became reality when she portrays herself as "alone, surrounded by my masks instead of the seven dwarfs, determined not to return home in shame after a failure that many had gleefully predicted, and [I] stubbornly continued on with my studies" (Diome, 2006, 26).

Indeed, several studies point to the fact that most immigrants' initial intentions are to return to their countries of origin. Although immigrants leave their countries of origin with specific goals and plans on how to achieve them, their plans are more likely to get derailed by the demands of their new realities. Research shows that this is particularly relevant for immigrants who have traveled long distances. Carling and Pettersen (2014, 14) suggest that "in fact, in the case of return migration, it is almost a rule of thumb that most migrants initially intend to return but often end up staying in the country of destination." The myth of return is well expressed by one respondent who said:

> Some got jobs with leading industries in their field, others got good jobs back in Kenya and had a good transition back into Kenya after years of being here.

Just like I (Konaté) struggled with the burning question of permanently returning home by weighing the advantages and disadvantages of such a life-altering decision on my future career and financial well-being, so have many of the participants in our study. Indeed, many immigrants go through that internal struggle because they have always entertained the idea of returning to their countries of origin once they had achieved the goals that they had set out when they emigrated to the West.

In his article titled, "'Mobile Transmigrants' or 'Unsettled Returnees'? Myth of Return and Permanent Resettlement among Senegalese Migrants," Giulia Sinatti (2011, 154) makes the following link between transnational migration and return back home:

> Characterised by a distinctive focus on mobility and movement, transnationalism depicts migration as a process that encompasses regular flows between countries. In its most simple terms, this perspective focuses on the increased interconnectedness between home and host countries engaged in by migrants, who maintain significant ties across national borders and live their lives simultaneously in multiple locations.

The emigration journey and the change of immigration status, along with adjustment of goals and expectations, can derail immigrants' initial goal of returning home. This is well described in the following respondent's experience:

> I came with a visitor visa. When I got married, I had another VISA type which was under my husband, a wife of a student. When he started working and had a working permit, I had a visa as the wife of someone who is working. From there, we went to get our permanent residence and then citizenship. To tell you the truth, at first, we didn't want to have citizenship of this country but of another one because of the way we were looking at this country. We were trying to find which country would be better to raise our children. So, it didn't matter to me.

One of the interviewees recounted the experience of a changed education trajectory:

> The program [Education exchange with universities] had set some expectations that I soon realized had to change. So, I achieved some and others I was not able to. I was enrolled in a four-year program, which I hoped to be done within 2 years and return home. But the content of the program changed so did its duration. This forced me to adjust the 2-year goal and be persistent to complete the program.

Another respondent described the dissonance and myth of going back home:

> I met a young girl from Zambia, and I don't know what to say. I know she studied; she was doing her master's degree. She was stalling, because if she graduated, she would have to go back to her home country but because she didn't want to go back she was stalling and she came to a point, she took all her classes, she was writing a paper and she kept on waiting so long writing this paper that finally all the classes that she took were not good anymore. They told her that she couldn't get a master's degree unless she started all over again because she took 3 or 5 years without graduating. After a certain number of years all the classes she took did not mean anything to them. She remained here, she couldn't have a master's degree and she was out of status so she couldn't go back.

This ambivalence that many sub-Saharan African immigrants experience is well captured by Mensah (2010, 153), who noted, "Although migrants would prefer permanent resettlement in the home country, their effective return strategies are the outcome of compromises made between return and the conflicting benefits offered by staying in migration." Mensah's two-decades-long research on the migration patterns of Senegalese immigrants in Canada suggests that although most Senegalese immigrants in Canada aspire to return to Senegal, the realities of their lived experiences in their host country make it difficult to fulfill that end goal. The myth of returning home "should no longer be exclusively conceived as permanent resettlement" but should also include "a variety of mobility patterns" or "'unsettled return,'" whereby some Senegalese immigrants go back and forth between Canada and Senegal (Mensah 2010, 154).

These contemporary patterns of transitory movements that African immigrants engage in between their host countries and their countries of origin have prompted Ammassari and Black (2001, 12) to suggest that migrations are not linear, and as such, we ought to conceptualize the desire of return home as not necessarily a "closure of the migration cycle, but rather" as "one of the multiple steps of a continued movement." "Return to the home country is understood as having an increasingly less permanent nature" in most contemporary studies about transnational migration patterns (Mensah 2010, 153).

Respondents interviewed for this project expressed the hope of completing school and going back to their countries of origin to improve their personal lives and support their families. When confronted by racism and discrimination, they devised coping methods. When those methods and strategies failed, they turned to courage and resilience and kept their hopes up. They treated the hardships they were experiencing as part of what foreigners must go through to achieve whatever success they had envisioned for themselves and their families. Some of their hopes and strategies included getting an education and going back home. One respondent stated:

> They just wanted me to have a certain level of higher education and be able to come home and help out financially. Be able to be somebody in a country, help out with something in the country.

Another said:

> They expect me to finish, graduate and go back. That has pushed me, been a motivating factor when I think about my husband and my children, and my mother. They are all waiting for me to finish with this doctorate and believe I can do it, has pushed me more.

An economic approach to the myth of going back home is too broad of a topic for this book to handle in depth. Research reports on how immigrants affect the economies of their host and home countries conducted by the Organisation for Economic Co-operation and Development (OECD 2014), by their Development Centre, and the International Labour Organisation (OECD/ILO 2018) found that some of the countries of origin heavily depend on these immigrants to support their citizens. While the immigrants are thinking that they are making a living and supporting themselves in the host country, they do not view it as contributing to the gross domestic product (GDP) of the host country. By sending some money back home and continuously supporting their families, the countries of origin are benefiting by having those citizens' lives uplifted and their well-being taken care of without the government's input. The sad thing about this approach is that immigrants struggle to make ends meet and still support their families back home as discussed earlier, yet they receive no recognition, appreciation or incentive for their contribution to the GDP of the host and home countries. The media has always been quiet about such issues, yet it has been very vocal in negatively politicizing immigration and immigrants.

The OECD Development Centre and the International Labour Organisation (OECD/ILO 2018) report base their research on three main dimensions of the economic contribution of immigrants in developing countries: labor markets, economic growth, and public finance. Data on its annual remittances by country, updated as of May 2021, show that those remittances sent through official channels had risen from $68 billion in 1990 to $553 billion in 2015. The report further records an increase rate to $640 billion in 2016 to $701 billion in 2020. This accounted for an average of 17 percent of GDP of most of the developing countries, which is more than the sum of all investments made by foreign companies to those countries and over triple the amount of aid governments of development partners provided in comparable years. Remittances are also more dependable than either international aid or investment, as discussed earlier. This goes to show that the myth of going back is more complex than the sentiments of sub-Saharan African immigrants feeling trapped by the inability to achieve their dreams and go back home.

Other respondents shared how they persisted and adjusted their plans as well as their expectations of America to succeed. This respondent's experience captures that struggle:

My life here has been very unsuccessful. I came here with intention of finishing my degree but got a lot of setbacks and I gave up on school and decided to work on meagre jobs to support my family.

The World Bank Group (2017) reported that remittances from migrant workers make up a significant proportion of GDP in many developing countries and have significant macroeconomic impact, as they serve as one of the major sources of income not only for the country but for many families. Donou-Adonsou et al. (2020) analyzed the top recipients of remittances as tracked by World Bank and IMF, and found that the two organizations underestimated the total flows since they only capture those sent through banks and money transfer operators.

The assistance sent by immigrants to their relatives, viewed by the immigrants as their sacrifice to support their families, is tracked by World Bank and other aid- and development-related organizations and accounted for in the GDP as remittances. The report shows that compared to official development aid or foreign direct investment given to some of the developing countries by their so-called development partners, immigrant remittances are more reliable, interest-free, and specific to the needs of the recipients.

Migrant remittances are defined by the (Wagh and Pattillo, 2007) and the OECD/ILO (2018) in terms of balance of payments by taking into consideration the gross earnings of workers who are living abroad for less than 12 months, some part of the compensation that the employees receive, monetary transfers sent home from those workers through officially recognized channels, and the net wealth transfers of those migrants who successfully navigate the immigration systems of their host countries (however long that takes, to earn permanent residence and eventually full-time employment). All these steps are accomplished by individual migrants without the assistance of either the host or the home countries.

This categorization and definition of what an immigrant is and what their role is in the host and home country fails to fully consider an immigrant as a fully participating member of the labor economic cycle. An immigrant like any other worker, if considered as a factor of production, human capital, as well as entrepreneur, contributes much more than just remittances to support family. An immigrant may arrive in the host country as a student and consumer, then transition into a worker and taxpayer, an entrepreneur a few years after graduation, an investor and huge community contributor in both countries within a decade.

In their research reports on remittances, Azizi (2020) and Ferreira et al. (2020) found that the impact on remittance-receiving countries when considered along with the issues of the outflow of migrants and inflow of remittances, can adversely affect remittance-receiving countries in terms of population, education, well-being, labor, capital, intellectual brain drain, poverty, and inequality. The researchers suggested the introduction of viable incentive savings or investment programs by host and home countries aimed at the senders of remittances.

This discussion on remittances and the implications thereof call for a redefinition of who an immigrant is, what their role is in the labor market, and most importantly their contribution to the GDP of both host and home countries. Celia Falicov (2007) decries the same issue and suggests an appreciation of the dynamics involved and relational implications of family life, relational stress that begins in the preparatory stages of migration, and acculturative stress manifested in gender and generational relationships after migration. Although the author's approach is clinical with a focus on family mental health therapy, Falicov (2007) examines the transnational activities and lifestyle, the myth of return, immigrants' intentions of going back home, and the complex influences of integration and acculturation in host countries with those of the adopted transnational lifestyle as they struggle to maintain connectedness to their countries of origin. She suggests the use of psychological and virtual families for therapeutic conversations that take the form of long-distance communication to maintain emotional, social and economic relationships via telephone calls, video chats and conferencing, email, and social media across continents.

This issue is complicated even further by the fact that some of the colonizing countries continue to burden the African continent with plundering and monetary policies that benefit them more than the continent. This approach continues to increase the already heavy debt burden that those countries have. For example, former African colonies of France continue to pay a "colonization tax" by having 50 percent of their foreign exchange in the French Public Treasury. These countries find themselves trapped by the French colonial francs monetary system. The CFA (Communauté Financière Africaine/African Financial Community) franc is a colonial currency that was created by France. It is made in Chamaniere, France, and managed by France.

The CFA franc zone consists of 14 countries in sub-Saharan Africa, each affiliated with one of two monetary unions. Benin, Burkina Faso, Côte D'Ivoire, Guinea-Bissau, Mali, Niger, Senegal, and Togo comprise the *West African Economic and Monetary Union*, or WAEMU, founded in 1994 to build on the foundation of the *West African Monetary Union*, founded in 1973. The remaining six countries—Cameroon, Central African Republic, Chad, Republic of Congo, Equatorial Guinea, and Gabon—comprise the *Central African Economic and Monetary Union*, or CAEMC. (IMF n.d.)

The currency is linked to the Euro, but has no parity to it, which makes it very hard for African countries to develop their economies because when one of the former French African countries export their goods to the West, they are bought with foreign currency and not in CFA francs. The French treasury automatically retains 50 percent of any sale of exported goods that its former African colonies make in foreign currency. The remaining 50 percent goes to the central bank of the former African colony. When any former French colony wants to import goods from another country, they have only the remaining 50 percent from the sale of their exported goods available for them to use. The currency conversion and exchange rate disadvantage the African country because they get a lower return.

This causes a structural problem that is at the root of not only the lack of development, but also the dependence of many African countries, who were colonized by France. As many of those African countries import more goods from the West than they export, they have less currency to be able to buy what they need. As a result, they perpetually borrow money from France at a higher interest rate and get a lower exchange rate, which perpetuates their economic dependence on their former colonial power. The money borrowed must in turn be paid in foreign currency, not in CFA francs. Thus, those countries get more and more in debt, while the potential of their economic development decreases. African countries are not the ones that decide the price of their raw materials. European countries that buy them fix the price. The African countries are thus at the mercy of the fluctuating prices that their buyers determine. Those raw materials are then manufactured in the West and turned into finished products, which are in turn sold back to African countries at much higher prices.

References

Al-Rasheed, M. 1994. "The Myth of Return: Iraqi Arab and Assyrian Refugees in London." *Journal of Refugee Studies* 7, nos. 2 and 3: 199–219.

Ammassari, S. and Black, R. 2001. Harnessing the Potential of Migration and Return to Promote Development: Applying Concepts to West Africa. United Nations.

Anwar, M. 1979. *The Myth of Return*. London: Heineman.

Azizi, Seyed Soroush. 2020. "Impacts of Remittances on Financial Development." *Journal of Economic Studies* 47, no. 3: 467–77.

Carling, Jørgen, and Silje Vatne Pettersen. 2014. "Return Migration Intentions in the Integration-Transnationalism Matrix." *International Migration* 52, no. 6: 13–30. https://doi.org/10.1111/imig.12161.

Diome, Fatou. 2006. *The Belly of the Atlantic*. London: Serpent's Tail.

Donou-Adonsou, Ficawoyi, Gyan Pradhan, and Hem C. Basnet. 2020. "Remittance Inflows and Financial Development: Evidence from the Top Recipient Countries in Sub-Saharan Africa." *Applied Economics* 52, no. 53: 5807–20, https://doi.org/10.1080/00036846.2020.1776834.

Falicov, Celia J. 2007. "Working with Transnational Immigrants: Expanding Meanings of Family, Community, and Culture." *Family Process* 46, no. 2: 157–71.

Ferreira, Joao-Pedro, Michael Lahr, Pedro Ramos and Eduardo Castro. 2020. "Accounting for Global Migrant Remittances Flows." *Economic Systems Research* 32, no. 3: 301–17.

IMF (International Monetary Fund). n.d. "The Fabric of Reform." An IMF Video. International Monetary Fund website. www.imf.org/external/pubs/ft/fabric/backgrnd.htm.

King, R. 2000. "Generalizations from the History of Return Migration." In *Return Migration: Journey of Hope or Despair?*, edited by B. Ghosh, 7–45. Geneva: United Nations and the International Organization for Migration.

Mensah, Joseph. 2020. "Home Sweet Home: Understanding the Geographies of Return Migration Intentions among Black Continental African Immigrants in Canada." *Canadian Ethnic Studies* 52, no. 3: 107–27.

Murphy, Eleanor J. and Ramaswami Mahalingam. 2004. "Transnational Ties and Mental Health of Caribbean Immigrants." *Journal of Immigrant and Minority Health* 6, no. 4: 167–78, https://doi.org/10.1023/B:JOIH.0000045254.71331.5e.

Nedelcu, Mihaela. 2012. "Migrants' New Transnational Habitus: Rethinking Migration through a Cosmopolitan Lens in the Digital Age." *Journal of Ethnic and Migration Studies* 38, no. 9: 1339–56, https://doi.org/10.1080/1369183X.2012.698203.

OECD (Organisation for Economic Co-operation and Development). 2014. *Is Migration Good for the Economy?* Migration Policy Debates 2. May 2014. Paris: OECD, www.oecd. org/els/mig/OECD%20Migration%20Policy%20Debates%20Numero%202.pdf.

———. 2016. *Perspectives on Global Development 2017: International Migration in a Shifting World.* Paris: OECD Publishing, http://dx.doi.org/10.1787/persp_glob_dev-2017-en.

———. 2017. *International Migration Outlook 2017.* Paris: OECD Publishing, http://dx.doi. org/10.1787/ migr_outlook-2017-en.

OECD/EU (Organisation for Economic Co-operation and Development/European Union). 2015. *Indicators of Immigrant Integration 2015: Settling In.* Paris/Brussels: OECD Publishing/European Union, http://dx.doi.org/10.1787/9789264234024-en.

OECD/ILO (Organisation for Economic Co-operation and Development/International Labour Organisation). 2018. *How Immigrants Contribute to Developing Countries' Economies.* Geneva/Paris: ILO/OECD Publishing, https://doi.org/10.1787/9789264288737-en.

Sinatti, Giulia. 2011. "'Mobile transmigrants' or 'unsettled returnees'? Myth of Return and Permanent Resettlement among Senegalese Migrants." *Population, Space and Place* 9, no. 2: 153–66.

Sirkeci, Ibrahim, Jeffrey H. Cohen, and Dilip Ratha. 2012. *Migration and Remittances during the Global Financial Crisis and Beyond.* Herndon, VA: World Bank Publications. https:// doi.org/10.1596/978-0-8213-8826-6.

Wagh, S. and Pattillo, C.A. 2007. *Impact of Remittances on Poverty and Financial Development in Sub-Saharan Africa.* Washington, DC: International Monetary Fund.

World Bank. 2019. "Record High Remittances Sent Globally in 2018." Press Release No. 2019/148. April 8, 2019. www.worldbank.org/en/news/press-release/2019/04/08/ record-high-remittances-sent-globally-in-2018.

World Bank Group. 2017. *Migration and Remittances, April 2017: Recent Developments and Outlook.* Migration and Development Brief, no. 27. Washington, DC: World Bank. https://openknowledge.worldbank.org/handle/10986/30278.

Zetter, R., 1999. "Reconceptualizing the Myth of Return: Contuity and Transition amongst the Greek-Cypriot Refugees of 1974." *Journal of Refugee Studies* 12, no. 1: 1–22.

Chapter 8

LEADERSHIP IN AFRICA AS A CONTRIBUTING FACTOR TO EMIGRATION

The challenges facing Africa not only stem from national and international policies but are also moral, spiritual, cultural, and even psychological in nature. While colonialism was devastating for Africa, it has become a convenient scapegoat for conflicts, warlordism, corruption, poverty, dependency, and mismanagement in the region. Africa cannot continue to blame her failed institutions, collapsed infrastructure, unemployment, drug abuse, and refugee crises on colonialism; but neither can these issues be understood fully without acknowledging the fact of Africa's past.

—Wangari Maathai

The main argument that the researchers are making in Chapter 8 is that current global leadership styles, specifically those found in Africa, and the disillusionment with leaders in some of the sub-Saharan African countries were the major immigration factors for some of the respondents. To give this chapter a historical and contextual baseline, the effect and impact that colonialism had and continues to have on Africa (and most of the world that experienced this trauma) will be discussed. The authors found that time has not healed all wounds, and the impact of colonialism still causes mental stress and continues to contribute greatly to low general well-being.

African leadership and management are areas that are not widely researched or publicized. What gets people's attention is negative coverage of issues which root cause is not fully investigated. Since African leadership and management was one of the emigration reasons cited by our respondents, we decided to research and find out more about the topic. We will examine the present and the past, and present a futuristic perspective on the issue. Additionally, we will discuss the issues related to Africa's identity, leadership, and management styles. These variables are important for Africa as they support the continent's self-determined evolution and leadership styles that will shape it beyond the twenty-first century. We argue that the discussion on African leadership and management demands a theoretical framework beyond Eurocentric models or one that sees Africa as a poor continent. We also avoid limiting the discussion on African leadership and management by solely looking at post or neocolonial history, the colonizers' conquest or savior stories, or by examining Africa as a monolithic culture ready for appropriation just like its human and natural resources.

To distinguish African leadership from Eurocentric leadership, Stella Nkomo (2011, 2) conducted research with a focus on "two questions: (1) How is 'African' leadership and management portrayed in organization studies literature? (2) What are the possibilities for re-writing 'African' leadership and management in organization studies?" Nkomo (2011, 7) reported that the "overall impression is the general scarcity of texts, materials and references to Africa in organization studies—it is largely invisible," and the resources available use and reinforce Western leadership and management knowledge to "examine 'African' leadership and management in the context of describing Africa's national culture primarily within Geert Hofstede's (1980) seminal typology or GLOBE's more current framework (House et al. 2004, 7)."

Expanding on our respondents' views on leadership as an immigration factor and global leadership framework and associated competencies, the authors explored and reviewed literature on African management leadership and philosophy studies by Africans. We found that most of them express the need for a framework beyond the now popularized Ubuntu, stating the inadequacy of Eurocentric and postcolonial frameworks to address Africa's current and future needs. Edoho (2001) approaches African management philosophy from a perspective that views it as a practical way of introducing and evaluating effectiveness in African governments, such as how they manage the vast wealth of the continent and take charge of the development and evolution process. Furthermore, the author evaluates African management philosophy by focusing on how business organizations become global and manage knowledge, skills, talent, and capital in a morally ethical manner. Most African leadership researchers argue that endogenous leadership and management systems need to be established and institutionalized, or else African leadership will continue to be evaluated using a Eurocentric model that does not account for Africa's uniqueness. Further, the models evaluate the new and evolving democracies of Africa according to the same criteria they use for mature democracies that have had centuries to evolve and self-determine, not to mention that they had Africa's resources at their disposal for their growth.

The renowned African philosopher Ali Mazrui (1980), when discussing the condition Africa found itself in during the 1960s to the 1980s, reflects on the question why Africa, now recognized as the earliest home of humans, is still not yet considered fit for human habitation. Further, comparing Africa with other societies that seem to have materially advanced, Mazrui questions the rationale behind slavery, colonization, South African apartheid, the poverty and food insecurity levels in a resource-rich Africa, continued massive brain drain, and the problem of refugees.

Up to today, the question of African democracy needing to be monitored remains unanswered. Without a clear criterion and a monitor with moral authority to do it, then who should be the watchdog? For decades, it has been the former colonizers that turned themselves into democratic watchdogs, although their own citizens accuse them of graft and human rights abuse. Instead of supporting African governments and their organizations and honoring the heads of states so that they can evolve and transform into acceptable democracies, there has been a continued demeaning and plundering just like in the days of colonialism. This process might have taken a different form, but the underlying goals are still the same if not more aggressive. It is this aggression of superpowers to take as much as they can from Africa that fuels conflicts in Africa. Some of the conflicts might be domestic, but the fire was lit elsewhere and is spreading. For decades, African Scholars like Ali Mazrui, Cheikh Anta Diop, Ngugi wa Thiong'o, and many more have decried the escalation of conflict into violence and civil war. The media was not helpful either. Wars in Europe and Asia that have lasted decades and issues of poverty and homelessness around the developed worlds get less media attention than low-scale civil wars and conflicts in Africa.

Ali Mazrui (1994, 40) further describes this relationship as one where the perpetrator has become a beneficiary of Africa's short memory of hate. Africans believe in peace and harmony and are not known to be as warlike and vindictive as their European and Western Counterparts. This is demonstrated by centuries of coexisting as multiethnic peoples without ever going to war in the scales recorded about Europe and Asia. Former prisoners detained by the colonizers, when set free, do not turn bitter and vindictive. Rather they focus on reconciliation and nation building, as was witnessed when the first President of Kenya, Jomo Kenyatta, and Nelson Mandela of South Africa were released, to mention only a few. A counterexample is that of Ian Smith who "in the old Rhodesia unleashed the horrors of UDI upon his people and was therefore instrumental in initiating a war in which many thousands of Africans were killed. When the war ended, he became a member of parliament of the new Zimbabwe and proceeded, quite often, to abuse the Black government of the day" (Mazrui 1994, 40).

The African Union recognizes that leadership and effective management is needed in Africa and notes that well-managed migration has the potential to benefit both the countries of origin and the destination countries. In its *Common Position*, the African Union (2006) identifies 11 priority issues, including migration and development, human resources and brain drain, labor migration, remittances, African diaspora, migration and peace, security and stability, migration and human rights, gender, children and youth, the elderly, and regional initiatives.

The issues that the authors wish to raise and focus on in terms of Africa's identity and self-determination is the freedom to exercise its own agency and power to chart its own evolution and transformation path on this planet. To return to the analogy we set out in Chapter 1 of Africa as a human being going through similar phases of evolution, growth, and transformation, we can now equate Africa to a young adult fresh out of college who needs to exercise freedom of choice and enjoy the lessons learned from mistakes and failures of actions that were personally and freely undertaken.

Our argument is that after the so-called departure of the colonizers and their settlers, Africa was never given a fair chance to recover from that trauma or supported for transformational reform and self-determination. Furthermore, the continent did not have the opportunity to reorganize, redefine, and eventually plan for its own development. Instead of receiving support, the plundering, dehumanizing, brainwashing, debt-burdening aid, self-serving development partners, and brain drain continue through the present. We posit that Africa has no development program of its own (or development direction) since most of the programming has always been tied to the demands of the former colonizers posing as donors and development partners.

The historical impact on Africans has been detrimental to their mental health as evidenced by the identity crisis created through naming systems and the cultural shifts discussed earlier, for example, the engagement of many Africans in depigmentation, as well as mass imitation of European values and ways of identifying the self and navigating life, including fashion, diet, and language among the major dimensions. This is the same pool of people from which we draw leaders who are expected to lead countries and global organizations.

As discussed in Chapter 1, sub-Saharan African immigrants are not adequately studied or given deserved media attention despite their major socioeconomic participation and contribution. Literature on sub-Saharan immigrants, including data from the African Union, indicates that there are larger migrant flows occurring within the continent than flows from African to non-African countries. In Chapter 1, we presented data showing how much sub-Saharan African immigrants contribute to the US economy while in Chapter 5 we showed with data how much they contribute to the economies of their countries of origin. This selfless category of Africans is hardly consulted on matter affecting Africa nor are they sourced for leadership positions.

The impacts of immigration and emigration on sub-Saharan African immigrants include reevaluating and redefining their identity and values, especially when they emigrate and experience living in cultures defined by highly politicized topics of migration, race, and the politics of global economics. Developing a transnational identity is not a mean task when coupled with a search for academic and economic success. Sub-Saharan African immigrants in the United States must do this all on their own, with no social or health resources from either their country of origin or host country. As noted earlier, the UNDP's Human Development Report of 2020 asserts that gross domestic product (GDP) is a crude indicator of economic achievements. What if reformed global governance from an approach of individual agency and human freedoms, tolerance and the realization of the full potential of every human life presently alive and future generations was allowed to be adopted in Africa?

Although international migration has become a major force of social transformation and globalization, issues of transnational identity, translanguaging, belonging, well-being, family dynamics and of course the high rates of brain drain from Africa are not mainstreamed in planning, policy and leader development. Researching this trend and its impact is challenging due to lack of data from countries of origin and the host countries. Even though most sub-Saharan African immigrants that the authors interviewed were beneficiaries of the F-1 visa, some were beneficiaries of the Diversity Visa lottery introduced in the 1990s. This indicates a trend of voluntary migration that bears some similarities to forced migration due to lack of economic opportunities, political reasons, poor governance and leadership in countries of origin. This is yet another aspect of migration that is not sufficiently studied.

While other continents facing development issues are given positive and encouraging labels (Asian Tigers, Flying Geese, etc.), Africa continues to be dehumanized and negatively labeled as the poor continent ridden with poor development predicaments and corruption, regardless of the well-known fact that it is a resource-rich continent, that is the envy and the cash cow of the superpowers. The real cause and source of its problems are never publicized through research or international reports. Being bombarded by superpowers with their competitive agendas, initiatives and programs that are always geared toward the enrichment of their home countries, is hardly a topic for researchers.

Given that the image of Africa in the international media is usually negative, what is leadership then in an African context? With today's leaders operating in a global context, can African leadership exist without global influence? Most advisors of African leaders seem to suggest that Africa find authentic African leadership styles (like Ubuntu) without considering Africa as part of the world. This perspective ignores a most crucial component of what leadership is: a fluid cultural construct whose meaning is embedded in the diverse cultures and expectations of the world. A leader's behavior and citizens' expectations of their leader are then derived from this definition. When assessing leadership, it is not the strength of character that is critical since this cannot operate in a vacuum. Rather it is the credibility and effectiveness of the institutions that the leader operates within that should be the concern of those assessing leadership and leader effectiveness. Credible and effective institutions at national and local levels will eliminate power rivalry that is placed at the very top of the hierarchy as the only lucrative position and model of leadership.

Other critical dimensions ignored by most leadership researchers include identity and nationalism issues. In Africa's young and multiethnic countries, the ethnic identity of a country's leader almost always influences citizens' national identity and level of patriotism as well as voter participation. That does not mean that there is no attachment to national identity, but it fluctuates. Ethnic solidarity has always been and remains strong and meaningful in Africa more than on other continents.

Tracing the history of African leadership demonstrates how challenging it is to be and live in Africa, let alone be a leader in Africa. Continued sources of conflict stemming from boundaries and values that were set by colonizers are always discounted and blamed on ethnic differences. Before colonization, issues of segregation, ethnicity, identity configuration, competitive resource ownership and control and border conflicts were never of the magnitude they are today, and anti-colonialism did not automatically translate into national unity and nationalism. In Africa, national identity must compete with people's ethnic identities, not economic and educational opportunities, as in developed countries.

Effects of Colonialism: Before the Wave of Freedom and Independence

The 1950s saw an increase in violence on the African continent. This was due to Africans becoming more vocal against colonial and apartheid rule. With most young African men being used by the colonizers in their wars abroad, these men indirectly learned how to wage war and how to plan and navigate strategically against enemies. They also learned how to negotiate for what they wanted. Struggle for freedom and the resulting wars unfortunately also saw an increase in despair, poverty and diseases, such as smallpox, as most agricultural activities were abandoned. Those left behind on the land, including women, the aging and children, were dying from hunger and poverty as much as the men were dying from war.

The 1960s became for Africa a period of redefining sovereignty, state and individual freedom. It also ushered in issues of self-governance, self-sufficiency and sustainability, as well as a consideration of what those issues meant for a continent plundered and left almost at the point of dying. In 1963, the Organization of African Unity was born. By 1977, almost all countries had fought and gained their independence except Zimbabwe, Namibia, and South Africa. However, this phase also brought unexpected challenges including managing borders between the new nations that were drawn by the colonizers based on their greed and plans for siphoning off African resources. These borders separated families and communities that had coexisted peacefully before colonization. It also brought together groups that were hostile to each other and were forced to not only coexist but also share a future together. This was the beginning of political ethnicity. Appointed and elected leaders now had yet another challenge on their agenda: uniting their nations and forging futuristic policies together.

Frantz Fanon (1968) analyzed and presented this issue aptly by defining and clarifying the intention of colonialism, predicated on the paradigms of difference and war, as destroying other civilizations and denying common humanity, as well as epistemicides, instead of finding ways to create a diverse world. Along the same lines, Ngugi wa Thiong'o (1986) gives it context by reframing the issue and the predicaments that were forcefully heaped on Africa by a much-ignored historical situation of colonialism and imperialism.

Undemocratic governance in Africa is a historical fact that has root causes in the ideological struggles between superpowers. United States policy toward Africa in the last 50 years, for example, promoted undemocratic governance and abuse of human rights, especially women and children, while preaching democracy and women's rights on the domestic front. After the Cold War, political figures and governments in Africa who agreed to be United States proxies in the struggle to contain Communism, saw their aid and support increase. This motivated other African countries to follow suit since they knew their sponsors would not hold them accountable. During apartheid rule in South Africa, the United States, and Europe continued doing business as usual with no regard for the impact that had on Africans.

United States presidents in the middle and late twentieth century were more interested in Africa as a resource (granary). Maybe only the one-term president saw Africa with a futuristic vision. President Jimmy Carter (1977–1981) argued that the chances of a successful African policy would be compromised unless there was a shift in goals (Carter's Foreign Policy 1977–1981). Further, the ultimate success of United States policy on Africa would depend on the quality of the United States' contribution to African development, helping Africa to develop in a peaceful direction without the focus on solving superpower confrontations and challenging Soviet intrusions into Africa.

Democratic reforms in Africa or anywhere in the world without transformation of government and proper checks and balances is futile. In Africa specifically, there is a need for limiting and curbing presidential and military rule. This has resulted in successful governance in some of the countries that have made an attempt toward transformation. Such countries have adopted hybrid political systems and power-sharing agreements like in the case of Liberia and Kenya among others. Divided government, although not necessarily federal like that of the United States, is also being adopted, with less reliance on central government so that in case of failure, it does not affect the governor and their constituents at the county levels.

The days when Africa was ruled by press releases, media censorship, presidential pronouncements, power concentrated in the executive branch with total disregard for the balance and separation of powers among the three branches are almost over. Most countries now are moving toward democracy through various levels of reforms, with decentralization and self-government at the county level becoming a favored power-sharing leadership style.

Military and constitutional coups remain problematic on our continent. Additionally, most of the 49 sub-Saharan African countries have presidential systems with power heavily concentrated in the hands of the president. Checks and balances remain a dream in most of our countries given the imbalance between the executive, legislative, and judiciary branches, as well as the imbalance between ruling parties and the opposition. Recent developments (military coups in Burkina Faso to the list Mali and Guinea and the constitutional coup in Chad) are good illustrations of much work we still have to do.

Several African countries have undertaken democratic reforms by revising and amending postcolonial constitutions, in some cases a total overhaul if not a complete redesign of constitutional order, revising strategies on the control of resources and moving away from patronage and citizen disfranchisement and economic marginalization with a focus on respect for the fiscal social contract. There is also increased scrutiny of social, economic and political costs associated with presidential supremacy and elections. Politicians are now heard addressing issues of too much dependence on foreign aid, remittances and international development partners instead of local production and taxes.

Lack of enthusiasm among the elite is understood, and there have been attempts to lure back some of them from wherever they are in diaspora. It is a difficult and challenging decision for this category of the diaspora given the history of imprisonment and exile for those elites who spoke out in the postcolonial decades.

The task of creating nation-states without resources or support from colonial plunderers and their religious puppets, or even the settlers who had benefited the most from the scramble for Africa, was a huge task for these inexperienced leaders. Devising a vision and mission that would drive a nation forward, heal it from the traumas of war and colonization and still create a space where the next generation could prosper became the mission of most of the newly independent state leaders. The leadership that was emerging was a hybrid of Eurocentric and Afrocentric styles. Whereas African styles were more communal, the Eurocentric ones were more cults of personality. The influence of Europe would never leave Africa. Some former leaders had expressed similar sentiments during their tenure:

> Sékou Touré of Guinea:
> Africa is fundamentally communocratic. The collective life and social solidarity give it a basis of humanism, which many peoples will envy. These human qualities also mean that an individual cannot imagine organising his life outside that of his family, village or clan [...]. The ability of intellectuals or artists, thinkers or researchers, is only valid if it coincides with the life of the people.
> —Sékou Touré, quoted in UNESCO General History of Africa, Volume VIII

That history of courage and resilience is almost often felt by immigrants when they find themselves confronted by similar systems wherever they emigrate. Most researchers of the period admire the way the continent found ways to make a rebound, give themselves frameworks for legitimacy and legality and to eventually become custodians of their own progress and destiny.

Post-Colonial and Effects of Coloniality

While most of the world has benefited and developed so fast from resources plundered from Africa, the continent continues to be impeded from self-determination and development. The continent has hardly benefited from the exploitative and highly competitive connection with the so-called developed world, perpetuated through development programs directed to the continent. The givers still take more than they give. The colonizers still enrich themselves and their citizens and develop their countries through the taxation of former colonies ongoing up to today. Researchers of the postcolonial period decry the loss of the gains made at independence and the intricate web of postcolonial factors that are hardly researched. They assert that the postcolonial rulers somehow, for lack of mentors and role models, started to imitate the colonial rulers. They were also under a lot of pressure by the citizens to deliver on their promises of cutting ties with the colonial rulers. Unfortunately, they soon found out that would not be easy.

Navigating a global world without resources and education became the biggest challenge and a reason for leaning on former masters. Decolonizing land, ecosystems and rights to resources, extricating them from the Crown Lands Ordinances, as well as addressing human rights were major issues that were made complex by the forced adoption of foreign leadership styles and education systems. Delegation after delegation visited their colonial masters' countries seeking assistance. To their horror, the assistance always came with stringent conditions that always affected the citizens adversely.

For example, the French and British colonial powers adopted two completely different administrative policies vis-à-vis their African colonies. While the British regarded its African colonies as separate entities from Great Britain and started to grant them independence as soon as they thought a given African colony was ready for self-autonomy, France viewed its African colonies as an extension of the French metropolitan. They were like overseas provinces of France. No wonder they are still paying taxes to France up to today. The 1946 French Constitution made the case of an indivisible union and increased the representation of its African colonies in the French Assembly. General De Gaulle's battle cry was that of "the republic, one and indivisible" after his 1958 election as president of France. As a result of its direct system of colonial administration, France's aim was to create a Franco-African "community" and not grant independence to its African colonies. Consequently, the French repressed with sheer brutality any attempt from their colonies to fight for independence. Under mounting pressures from several of their African colonies, France organized a referendum in its West African colonies in September 1958 and invited Africans to vote either yes or no to stay under "French Union."

Sékou Touré, the president of Guinea, had been asking for independence since 1956. Guinea was the only West African colony that voted to break away from the French Union, and thus gained its independence in 1958. France was surprised by the decision and decided to punish Guinea to serve as a lesson to any of their other colonies that might want to follow in Guinea's steps. The French withdrew all their personnel, including the office equipment and telephones. They also destroyed roads and railways, and were responsible for the mass destruction of infrastructure, schools, public administration buildings, health facilities, research institutes, agriculture and other resources. Only a £10 million loan that Kwame Nkrumah, then president of Ghana, granted to Sékou Touré saved it from total collapse. Guinea's independence inspired many other West African French colonies to demand their independence from France. Many gained their independence in 1960. Assistance from and within the continent by the continent member states and wealthy individuals, as demonstrated here, can go a long way in making Julius Nyerere's (first president of independent Tanzania) dream of creating self-reliant citizens and African nations come true.

Structural adjustment programs (SAPs) with their myopic and micro approach to women, youth and children's issues, administered and supervised by the World Bank, IMF, UN, and African Economic forums, have caused most African leaders to feel like their hands were tied and a gun held to their heads to accept the terms and conditions of these programs. Excerpts from the speeches of the late former president of Burkina Faso Thomas Isidore Noël Sankara (Top 20 Thomas Sankara Quotes 2018) indicate how most leaders felt at that time:

Debt is a cleverly managed reconquest of Africa.

He who feeds you controls you.

Imperialism is a system of exploitation that occurs not only in the brutal form of those who come with guns to conquer territory. Imperialism often occurs in more subtle forms, a loan, food aid, blackmail. We are fighting this system that allows a handful of men on earth to rule all of humanity. Under its current form, that is imperialism-controlled, debt is a cleverly managed re-conquest of Africa, aiming at subjugating its growth and development through foreign rules. Thus, each of us becomes the financial slave, which is to say, a true slave.

Regardless of the harsh conditions and terms that came with SAPs and other development aid to Africa, there seemed to be a general leadership culture that was developing where the ruling Africans formed an elitist kind of club. Major characteristics that were evident across newly freed colonies included using the sovereignty of the postcolonial African state for their own individual benefits or withholding benefits from those they deemed to be competitors (dissidents as they called them) thereby leaving the masses in desperate living and economic conditions. Most of the researchers of the period who publicly spoke against their governments were eliminated, imprisoned or exiled. Others self-exiled to avoid the harsh treatment that they witnessed across the continent meted out on those who attempted to educate the masses.

Many Firsts: Female Presidents in Africa

Women have been sidelined and excluded from leadership since the colonial period. This phenomenon, which is un-African, caused a lot of strain not just in state leadership but all the way to grassroots movements and within families. Where women tried to negotiate those political spaces, they were always met with forceful resistance by state security. Environmentalist and Nobel Peace Prize winner Wangari Maathai of Kenya was one such woman that faced the harshest treatment from her country's leadership for educating women to be self-sufficient and for leading demonstrations against the plundering of natural resources, especially deforestation.

African female political leaders are presented in a negative way by the international media, which calls into question their credibility as leaders of their nations even when democratically elected. In acknowledging this media blackout, Ellen Johnson Sirleaf (2009), former president of Liberia, and 2011 Nobel Peace Prize winner, wrote in her memoir:

> At least 250 African women have been recorded by the West in their historical records as having been prominent leaders as presidents, vice presidents, ministers, prime ministers [...] and [ministers of military and defense].

Africa has the most female presidents and government leaders of any continent. There does not even exist an English word to describe female leaders and warriors except as a derogatory remark about them being man-like. While India's first female president, the first female president in the world, was elected in 1934, Africa's first was not elected until 1945, if you recognize Sarah Jibril's candidacy and political role (Sarah Nnadzwa of Kwara State in Nigeria) and other Queen warriors. Before colonization, most communities described their female warriors with adjectives that were also used for men because they were seen as warriors and not women. Their valor was no less just because they were women. With colonization, all that changed. For example, the famous female warrior queens and all female regimental armies that defeated colonizers like the French in West Africa were belittled by having Eurocentric sexist terms and insults thrown at them.

We will always remember and celebrate female warrior Queen Nzinga, who fought the Portuguese in 1640. Ana Nzinga Mbande was queen of the Ndongo and Matamba kingdoms in modern-day Angola. She was a skilled politician and diplomat who successfully negotiated treaties first with the Portuguese, then with the Dutch. She was also an excellent military tactician, launching repeated skirmishes against the Portuguese between 1644 and 1657, until they requested a new peace treaty.

Kaipkire was a warrior and female chief of the Herero tribe of modern-day Namibia. She is remembered for leading her people in many battles against British slave traders in the 1700s. Mekatilili Wa Menza, a charismatic, well-loved and respected warrior queen of Kenya has many songs and poems in her name that I (Fredah) remember singing growing up and later using the poems to teach African poetry, all in preservation of her memory. She is most celebrated for defending traditional ways of life and calling out the hypocrisy of the British settlers who stole Giriama land and forced her people to work on it almost for free, since most of their pay went to exorbitant taxes and hut fees. Princess Sarraounia of Niger is remembered for the support she got from her father, becoming a warrior who fought and defeated the French, and eventually became a queen warrior at a very young age.

Records about female leadership in Africa are not well documented, and a brief literature review will quickly bring this to light (Madimbo 2016). Modern records show the first female president in Africa as Sylvie Kinigi, with no reference to Sarah Jibril. She was the prime minister of Burundi from February 10, 1993 to October 7, 1994. However, some leaders are not recognized by colonizers and therefore not recorded, while others, unless elected and not assuming office to fill a vacuum, are not recognized. For example, Ruth Sando Fahnbulleh Perry was known for being the first female president of Liberia and in contemporary Africa as a whole, yet Ellen Johnson Sirleaf holds that record. Perry died on January 8, 2017 at the age of 77. Sarah Jibril, born Sarah Nnadzwa at Kwara State in Western Nigeria, was also not recognized as a leader, and her political career and role played in pre-independence Nigeria is not fully recorded.

Here are other female giants of Africa: In 1993, Agathe Uwilingiyimana of Rwanda, sometimes known as Madame Agathe, served as prime minister and acting president until her assassination in 1994, during the opening stages of the Rwanda genocide. Uwilingiyimana's leadership, reconciliation strategies and conflict resolution among the major ethnic groups won her favor with East African leaders. She also became a pioneer in women's rights and education in Rwanda.

Fast forward to 2021: Tanzania elected their former vice president, Samia Suluhu Hassan, as the first female president, after the death of President John Magufuli. 2021 also saw Fadumo Dayib, become the first female presidential candidate in Somalia's history. In 2020, Togo elected their first female prime minister, Victoire Sidémého Dzidudu Dogbé Tomegah, who was previously the Minister of Grassroots Development, Handicrafts, Youth and Youth Employment. Rose Christiane Ossouka Raponda is currently serving as the first female prime minister of Gabon since July 2020 and was previously the country's defense minister.

Ameenah Gurib-Fakim became the first female president of Mauritius from 2015 to 2018. She was selected to be a presidential candidate in 2014 following the resignation of then president Kailash Purryag, and was unanimously elected president by the National Assembly. Although a ceremonial position, in 2018 Ethiopia elected Sahle-Work Zewde as the first elected female president to work with Prime Minister Abiy Ahmed Ali.

In 2006, Liberia elected Ellen Johnson Sirleaf for two consecutive terms, making her the first female elected president. Previously she had run for presidency against Charles Taylor and lost in 1997. Her other leadership roles included being elected chair of the Economic Community of West African States in June 2016. The year 2009 saw Rose Francine Rogombé serve as interim president of Gabon after the death of President Omar Bongo. As president of the Senate at that time, she automatically became the head of state. Rogombé died on April 10, 2015, at the age of 72.

The year 2012 gave us Joyce Hilda Banda, the president of Malawi from April 7, 2012 to May 31, 2014. She is an educator and grassroots women's rights activist. Previously, she was the vice president of Malawi from May 2009 to April 2012 and minister of foreign affairs from 2006 to 2009. Cissé Mariam Kaïdama Sidibé is the first woman to be appointed to the position of prime minister in Mali's history. She was assistant to the minister beginning in 1987. Aminata Touré, dubbed Iron Lady during her tenure because of her anti-corruption campaign, was the second female prime minister of Senegal from September 1, 2013 to July 4, 2014. She previously served as justice minister from 2012 to 2013. She holds a PhD in international financial management with a focus on microfinancing women in sub-Saharan Africa.

Catherine Samba-Panza, a corporate lawyer, was the first female to hold a head of state role as an acting head of state of the Central African Republic from 2014 to 2016. Previously she was the mayor of the capital city Bangui.

Other female presidents that we don't hear about include Ivy Matsepe-Cassaburi who served temporarily as the acting president of South Africa when the president and the vice president were out of the country for four days in September of 2005. Agnes Monique Ohsan Bellepeau was the acting president of Mauritius from March 31, 2012 to July 21, 2012, and again from May 29, 2015 to June 5, 2015. Other high-level leadership positions held by women include Cécile Manorohanta who has been Madagascar's deputy prime minister for the interior since 2009.

Present Times in Africa

Economic dependence on former colonial masters and current imperialists continues to plague the African continent. The connection between dependence and the breakdown of indigenous sociocultural values is not to be taken lightly. When a family cannot provide and protect the next generation, they cannot consider themselves free, and they cannot easily define who they are as a people. One's identity in such a situation is tied to the economic provider or enabler of the situation. Postcolonial foundations that were laid then still affect the continent today. From education systems and religious affiliations, to health and financial systems including the media, the language of instruction in schools and the skewed global relations, systems that continue to benefit the colonizers and imperialists also continue to demean the sovereignty and identity of the African continent.

Most leadership studies argue that the greatest purpose of good leadership should be to benefit the whole society through programs and structures that assist in the refining and improving of communities and the individuals that belong to said country or state. Unfortunately, this is not the case even in the so-called developed worlds, and the main reason offered was poor communication. What is lacking in most of those so-called developed worlds is uncensored mass media, as well as leadership development programs whose curriculum is grounded in a commitment to the citizens (Ncube 2010; Madimbo 2016; Adeniran Adebusuyi and Ikuteyijo 2017).

In his logical framework on sub-Saharan African leadership, Michael Muchiri (2011) argues that since leadership is defined from a contextual perspective, contextual factors of societal culture, citizens' behaviors and patrimonial behaviors in sub-Saharan Africa are not factored into most leadership studies. The tendency for African leaders to imitate foreign leadership styles, instead of developing their own based on community needs and cultural values, is prevalent. This creates a precedent where the next generation of leaders is not only influenced by but also inherits this flawed leadership framework. It also creates a leadership style that has no context in Africa except for the negative and traumatic impacts of colonial factors that have influenced citizens and their definition of who a leader is.

United States Policy toward Africa

Once again [...] shown the key contributions that migrants make in keeping our societies functioning. During the confinement, foreign-born workers were highly represented in essential activities such as health care and food retail and in some of the hard jobs that the native born eschew, such as picking fruit. Even when travel and admission were severely restricted, most countries realised they needed to make exceptions for some migrants in these sectors.

Migrant workers are on the frontline of the COVID-19 crisis: in the health sector, they account for 24% of medical doctors and 16% of nurses. More broadly, as discussed in the special chapter of this publication, "The Role of Migration in Shaping Industry Structure," migrants are overrepresented in domestic services, the cleaning industry, seasonal agricultural work, and the transportation sector. Their contributions to these sectors should at least be recognised, if not rewarded.

In the United States, for example, in the year to August 2020, the unemployment rate for the foreign-born jumped from 3.1% to 10.2%, while it increased from 3.9% to 8.1% for the native born. (OECD 2020)

The preferences of the average citizen appear to have a very low, almost insignificant impact on public policy regardless of broad support for the issue being put to the vote. The Africa Command (AFRICOM) was declared a fully unified command in October 2008. At the time of its inception, one of its core aims was to forge closer collaborative links between civil and military aspects through the United States policy toward Africa as an improvement from those policies of since the time of major world wars. Then United States president George W. Bush declared that AFRICOM would enhance United States efforts in bringing peace and security to the people of Africa while promoting common goals of development, health, education, democracy and economic growth in Africa.

Since then, there is no evidence of the stated outcomes for Africa, yet United States economic, political and, above all, security interests in or associated with the African continent are still in place and benefiting the United States at the expense of poor Africans. Oil and other raw materials, such as cobalt, make up more than one-fifth of United States imports that already come from Africa. What has Africa got? More debt and increased insecurity perpetrated on the continent while being targeted by the United States in terms of a decrease in foreign aid, partisan politics, negative media coverage, and more competitors vying for her resources just as in the days of Scramble for Africa and the post-Cold War era. As for Europe, you would expect that it would increase its support of the continent it colonized and continues to benefit from. However, its aid has continued to decline, especially in the last three decades. As for competitors, there is an increased presence of Brazil, India and Russia, with China in particular becoming Africa's second most important trading partner after the United States (Gramby-Sobukwe 2005; Gänzle 2011; Migration Policy Institute 2012; OECD 2020).

The late president of Burkina Faso Thomas Isidore Noël Sankara (Top 20 Thomas Sankara Quotes, 2018) comes to mind again in his fight for equality and women's empowerment:

> The revolution and women's liberation go together. We do not talk of women's emancipation as an act of charity or out of a surge of human compassion. It is a necessity for the revolution to triumph. Women hold up the other half of the sky.
> Comrades, there is no true social revolution without the liberation of women. (Women Equality and Rights by Thomas Sankara. https://youtu.be/6bTTM7rlnfg)

African leaders are not always their own self-made leaders or in leadership to serve their people. Rather, having learned from their predecessors, who had learned from their colonial masters, they continue to use the institutions of state power as repressive weapons against the people to service the leaders' own personalistic interests.

Characteristically, they impose three conditions that severely undermine democracy. First, the state becomes an instrument of authoritarian control. Police and the military are used to target the people to ensure compliance or to accumulate rents in the absence of state wages and solidify state domination. Second, a weak and ideologically divided society is sustained by fostering political ethnic factionalism. Third, elites are co-opted by offers of individual gain to foment the factionalism that weakens civil society (Bolden and Kirk 2009).

The self-imposed United States role in the world had been to act as the standard for democracy and best global leadership, an example of best defense and military prowess including space exploration, leader in the promotion of the liberal international order and defender and promoter of freedom, democracy and human rights, among others. After 9/11, United States policy toward Africa focused on United States national security interests and away from the usual low-level democratic and development interests, a signal that Africa was becoming less important as a development partner. This has become even clearer since the start of the COVID-19 pandemic.

A paradigm shift is needed for Africa to become a mature leader without imitating others. People are looking for the most effective person and their best behaviors or the most effective method to lead. As long as the leadership remains in its current formulation, leadership and leader development will always be limited. Manipulative and narcissistic leaders and followers have been passing through this sieve of Eurocentric leadership into organizations and nations for centuries. Research in this area is lacking both an integration of the diverse concepts and a comprehensive framework for a workable definition of leadership in the twenty-first century and beyond.

On current leadership characteristics, Mainah and Perkins argue that "although this may have been true in the past, especially in times of war, or may even be true today in times of combating terrorists, there are many other and clearly better ways to develop self-esteem and self-confidence, and to support organizational success without the negative impacts of narcissism" (Mainah and Perkins 2015, 6).

On suggestions and solutions for African leadership, most researchers recommend a search for endogenous leadership and management systems and a framework that best suits Africa's unique history and resources. Edoho (2001, 74) offers suggestions and defines African management philosophy as, "The practical way of thinking about how to effectively run organizations—be they in the public or private sectors—based on *African* (emphasis mine) ideas and in terms of how social and economic life is actually experienced in the region. Such thinking must be necessarily interwoven with the daily existence and experience in Africa and its contextual reality."

Other researchers had more questions than answers, wondering if indigenous "African" leadership and management could be reclaimed and reinstitutionalized in Africa. African management philosophy scholars argue that Eurocentric practices are inadequate because leadership and management challenges in Africa are embedded in a very different cultural, political, economic, and social context. Incorporating Ubuntu principles in management were seen as a possibility to introduce humaneness into leadership and to increase Africa's competitive advantage. Even our respondents offered no answers because they had their own questions and conflicting thoughts:

That's a long story. I came two times, I came at the age of 18 through American Exchange, this is for one-year, good high school students were brought here, and Ethiopia was a participant. There were many African countries as well. I was selected from my secondary school after I finished the eleventh grade going to twelfth I was taken for one year. For the first time in 1969, I spent in Southern California in a town called Chula Vista in the high school as a senior. That was transforming, from rural Ethiopia and at term from the entire country including Eritrea there were 25 people selected. I was selected from my Province and from Eritrea there were two. Then I had to go back, went to university the first year was fine and then the second year a revolution broke out and it was difficult. So, I got that link and tried to make it on my own, got some American people to help me in 1971 and I came here in August of that year.

[...] the whole idea of going back to Nigeria had been thrown out ,
it was no longer feasible and even colleagues at home that I had worked
with you know in the university system before I came were telling me
things were not as it was in the '80s you know when I left Nigeria.
So you know I should stay here if I have the opportunity to build
a career in the United States.

I was basically searching for opportunities with intention of finishing
and then going back but we had a dictator from '74 to '91 and that
was very difficult for Ethiopians. Ethiopians left after '74 because of
abuse of power. The U.S abandoned Ethiopia despite good relations
during the Regan area on education, defense, that's the history.

My experience in Nigeria would be that I have to confront ethnic
discrimination. We have about 250 languages in Nigeria so that is a
different experience and then coming here I have never up to the time
I came to north america, Canada and us, I have never confronted
racial discrimination in high school. I had Irish reverend fathers as my
teachers, British Council teachers, American Peace Corp volunteers;
the relationship was not based on race. We were more in terms of what can
I benefit from my teacher. And in fact, my going to Canada in 1989
for my doctoral work was based on interaction I had with a Canadian
professor who came to the university where I was teaching with my MA.
He was my head of department for a year he was a visiting professor
and so when he was going back he said he would like some of us to
come to his university. They found a host university in Canada to do
a PhD with him. So, he was a White man who was very much interested
in giving young Africans a good education and I ended up getting
a four year's PhD scholarship and not only myself, there was another
Nigerian who was on the program. He was also on the same scholarship
with me. So, in 1993 when we graduated, we were three Nigerians and
one Canadian who worked under two White Canadian professors
in the department. So to that extent one cannot always talk about
racism in relation to Whites but in the larger North American society
there is really the problem of racism. So, you can't ignore that and
so when you now look at that in terms of the experience of African
Americans in the United States we as Africans our experiences are very
different. I grew up in a society where no one can tell you that you can't
make it. Yes, there was ethnic discrimination, you might apply for a job
in Nigeria and if you don't belong to the majority ethnic group you
might not get the job but that is not to say that anybody puts you down
to say you can't make it if one [...] . . but for African Americans they
really don't have the choice. Like in my case I could easily have gone

back to Nigeria to take up a faculty appointment so that makes it a little bit different. You know for African Americans this is the only country that they know and when they are discriminated against they really don't have a choice to. I can see why many seem as angry and upset with the racial discrimination in society.

One of our respondents wished he could go back home and become a better leader than he was witnessing:

I was hoping to be done with my PhD and go back to Africa as an elite politician and become president.

African Leadership in the Twenty-first Century and Beyond

When survival of the fittest appears to be synonymous with evolution, physical dominance appears to characterize evolution.
—Adapted from Gary Zukav

From this discussion and our findings, we agree with most researchers of sub-Saharan African leadership that there is an urgent need to redefine leadership and power, especially in sub-Saharan Africa (Edoho 2001; Louw 2002; Bennett et al. 2003; Mbigi 2005; Obiakor 2005; Chhokar et al. 2007; Cameron 2014; Gumede 2017). Beyond colonial influence on their leadership, patrimonial and Ubuntu cultural aspects that are unique to Africa are mostly ignored in the literature on African leadership.

The common Eurocentric trait theory of leadership does not work anymore. The one alpha-male-leader type of leadership has slowly been replaced by a collaborative and transformational leadership style where shared responsibility toward a goal bigger than the founders and leaders is the guiding vision and mission. Some successful tech and financial companies are leaderless with self-managing teams and are doing great in their sectors.

Enrollment in traditional brick-and-mortar leadership programs might start declining as the general trend currently favors virtual learning. Online leadership master classes, however, have seen an increase in followers and registrants, which they owe to social media. Some organizations now have their internal "lead from where you are" programs that are customized to the needs of the organization. We guess there is a new realization that most employees have leadership potential and personal power, and that the pyramidal triad structure is not built with the ability or capacity to provide empowerment in those structural positions. The same goes for leadership in countries. Citizens have leadership potential, and their own leaders need not imitate foreign styles.

Structural power can be taken away at the will of organizational leadership, not so personal power. Centuries of deliberately setting up control and command systems and leadership personalities that quell personal power have resulted in the realization that it does not work. The bottom-line days are also gone when financial results were the only or primary measure on which a business's success was judged and celebrated. GDP and gross national product are also no longer the best measure of a country's economic might and success, as discussed in an earlier chapter. Today and in the future, organizations will be assessed beyond the triple bottom line, on topics like how they manage multigenerational aspects of their organization, multicultural values and ways of communicating, emerging technologies, young millionaires (We have crypto billionaires who are just out of their teen years!) who are self-driven and willing to participate (unlike baby boomer millionaires who were self-engrossed because they had made it), as well as the impact they have on the social and physical environment and on their customers and the people who work for and with them. Social media is their boardroom and not some secret location with heavy security to ensure only the invited attend.

What was often described as a challenge of shifting demographics is now a norm and a common organizational feature. The pyramidal triad and silo structure of organizations has already been replaced by self-managed virtual team leadership. Management by objectives and walking around is so archaic. It is hilarious even to think of it as a leadership style. The water cooler corner is empty. Chat rooms and intranet social media have replaced it. The landline might still be hanging on its hook but hardly rings because it has been replaced by mobile devices.

Researchers' Reflection: Fredah Mainah, PhD

I remember in graduate school having an argument with a White male leadership course professor because I said that no organization succeeds through the efforts of one person. As such, celebrating one leader (Man of the Year) was not realistic. I appreciate the fact that entrepreneurs risk a lot of their assets, but they do not become millionaires or billionaires all by their personal risk. The professor was a staunch follower of trait and one-male patriarchal leadership theory. I am more of a transformational and participative leader and so espouse inclusivity, collaborative kind of joint leadership, collective consciousness and accountability.

I made my argument by referencing how when things go wrong internally, the leader is never blamed or questioned, despite the fact that the employees were implementing his so-called organizational mission and strategies, which are linked either to the leader or founders. The board members and shareholders are also never implicated in blame or held accountable.

Therefore, the idea of some people individually making it to the list of the top millionaires or billionaires is also ridiculous. They did not mobilize those resources and increase them exponentially all by themselves. Some space billionaires, although in a condescending kind of tone that attracted social media backlash, acknowledged and thanked their employees and customers for getting them to space. No mission that is expected to be bigger than one person can be achieved by one solo individual. Given this level of unappreciated effort, it is no wonder that there is such employee turnover and low morale, coupled with high levels of stress and burnout in C-suite positions.

In this century and beyond, anyone Computers are no longer the main medium for accessing information. Anyone with a smartphone can access loads of information available on whatever topic that interests them. That also means that they can participate from their cell phone in demanding information that was traditionally unavailable to the so-called general public or citizen. Where there is unfairness or unjust systems or processes, the public and especially the youth can demand rectification and justice.

The youth are one group continuously left out of the decision-making processes even when the issues affect them. By 18, they are expected to vote (not drink yet) and yet not be involved in the issues they are voting on or question the face representing the issue. When the youth raise their voices, even on global problems, there is always a grown-up shutting them down and demeaning their passion (if not shooting at them with real guns) because of their youthful age.

The times when one had to wait until 50 to become a millionaire drew to a close two decades ago. Teenagers have been known to become millionaires. The majority of millionaires today are younger than 30 years of age. It is no longer surprising to see a CEO under 30, which was unheard of for the longest time. Even in civil service, the face of leadership in most of the agencies has changed and no longer do most top leaders fit the typical description of the old male.

Organizations preach about authentic leadership and empowered employees with very little understanding of what that is, just like they do with diversity. Authenticity has a lot to do with personal power emanating from genuine reverence for every life, not respect, tolerance, or acceptance, which derive from characterizing and judging. Whether leading a company or a country, leadership from a personal place of genuine reverence for every life is authentic and equips one with the capabilities of deep respect and honoring other beings without seeing diversity except in its beautiful variety.

We have seen a lot of disruption not just in leadership and management, but also in technology (which played a great part in that process), especially during the COVID-19 crisis. For example, traditional brick and mortar banks were already seeing fewer customers in their banking halls and fewer new account requests before COVID-19. This is because of their online banking functions, self-service and automated services and apps. Peer-to-peer lending and other ways for requesting and sending funds via the Internet by use of free apps was taking off and becoming popular. This has now replaced a huge chunk of investment and venture capital. Apps where there are neither middlemen, nor fees and commissions have liberated and democratized the traditional way of accessing money and cash, trading (buying and selling) and more importantly investing. Small one-person businesses can now grow to organizations worth billions through cloud fund raising, without the rigorous and lengthy processes involved in accessing loans the traditional way.

Postcolonial African leaders, therefore, need to rethink their leadership and political strategies in Africa. There is an increase in literature calling for a redefinition of leadership and a reengagement with indigenous knowledge and practices and their potential use for leader development. In their critical constructionist argument for developing an Afrocentric leadership perspective and leader development programs in the region of sub-Saharan Africa, Bolden and Kirk (2009) propose the promotion of relational activities, dialogue and experience sharing, "self in community" and transference of indigenous leadership practices and knowledge, as new ways of gaining leadership understanding. This, they suggest, would be a positive step toward leader development programs and activities that develop leadership behaviors and competencies geared toward diversity and cross-cultural management and inclusive leadership. From these arguments, the authors have dedicated the next chapter to investigate the role of leader development in an attempt to improve African leadership.

Preferred leadership styles in and for Africa include a hybrid of participative and humane approaches, cultural interaction, solidarity, and interdependence (Edoho 2001; Mbigi 2005; Obiakor 2005; Bolden and Kirk 2009; Nkomo 2011; Cameron 2014; Gumede 2017). In their exploratory study on perspectives of leadership in Africa, Senaji et al. (2014) found that preferred leadership styles included humorous leaders with vision, who are inspiring and at the same time committed to national goals, who are guided by a high level of honesty and transparency, and sensitive to normative differences. Leader development systems must nurture leaders who are capable of dealing with the institutional and organizational ills that imperil the continent and constrain the achievement of Africa's development potential.

Most literature reviewed suggested approaching leadership as fundamentally a process of sensemaking and leadership development as a means by which participants can reframe their understandings of troublesome leadership issues including control and dependency to create alternative narratives and practices (Bolden and Kirk 2009). This is a galactic and transformative shift from functional and transactional approaches of leadership as an alienating social myth that is highly centralized and bureaucratic. This has historically been used especially in Africa to maintain status relationships and legitimize the unequal distribution of power and resources. This approach challenges the embedded colonial and imperialistic assumptions in current leadership styles and leader development programs.

References

Adeniran Adebusuyi, Issac and Lanre Ikuteyijo. 2017. *Africa Now! Emerging Issues and Alternative Perspectives*. Cham: Springer International Publishing.

African Union. 2006. *African Common Position on Migration and Development*. Executive Council, Ninth Ordinary Session. 25–29 June 2006. Banjul, The Gambia. www.iom.int/sites/g/files/tmzbdl486/files/jahia/webdav/shared/shared/mainsite/microsites/rcps/igad/african_common_position_md.pdf.

———. n.d. *The Revised Migration Policy Framework for Africa and Plan of Action (2018–2027), Draft*. https://au.int/sites/default/files/newsevents/workingdocuments/32718-wd-english_revised_au_migration_policy_framework_for_africa.pdf.

African Union Commission. 2015. *Agenda 2063: The Africa We Want*. Framework Document. September 2015. https://au.int/sites/default/files/documents/33126-doc-framework_document_book.pdf.

Ake, Claude. 1996. "Rethinking African Democracy." In *The Global Resurgence of Democracy*, edited by Marc F. Plattner and Larry Diamond, 63–75. 2nd ed. Baltimore, MD: Johns Hopkins University Press.

Bennett, Nigel, Christine Wise, Philip A. Woods, and Janet A. Harvey. 2003. *Distributed Leadership*. Nottingham: National College of School Leadership.

Bolden, Richard and Philip Kirk. 2009. "African Leadership: Surfacing New Understandings through Leadership Development." *International Journal of Cross Cultural Management* 9, no. 1: 69–86.

Cameron, Gail. 2014. *Authentic African Leadership*. Houghton: Real African.

Carter's Foreign Policy 1977–1981. https://history.state.gov/departmenthistory/short-history/carter

Chhokar, Jagdeep S., Felix C. Brodbeck, and Robert J. House. 2007. *Culture and Leadership across the World: The GLOBE Book of In-depth Studies of 25 Societies*. London: Routledge.

Collier, Paul. 2008. *The Bottom Billion: Why the Poorest Countries Are Failing and What Can Be Done about It*. New York: Oxford University Press.

Coughlan, Sean. 2006. "All You Need is Ubuntu." *BBC News Magazine*. Accessed September 28, 2006. http://news.bbc.co.uk/2/hi/uk_news/magazine/5388182.stm.

Davidson, Basil. 1991. *African Civilization Revisited*. Trenton, NJ: Africa World Press.

Diop, Cheikh Anta. 1987. *Pre-colonial Black Africa*. Westport, CT: Lawrence Hill and Company.

Edoho, Felix M. 2001. "Management in Africa: The Quest for a Philosophical Framework." In *Management Challenges for Africa in the Twenty-first Century: Theoretical and Applied Perspectives*, edited by Felix M. Edoho, 73–89. Westport, CT: Praeger.

Fanon, Frantz. 1968. *The Wretched of the Earth*. New York: Grove Press.

Gänzle, Stefan. 2011. "AFRICOM and US Africa Policy: 'Pentagonising' Foreign Policy or Providing a Model for Joint Approaches?" *African Security Review* 20, no. 1: 70–82.

Gordon, April. "The New Diaspora-African Immigration to the United States." *Journal of Third World Studies* 15, no. 1: 79–103.

Gramby-Sobukwe, Sharon. 2005. "Africa and U.S. Foreign Policy: Contributions of the Diaspora to Democratic African Leadership." *Journal of Black Studies* 35, no. 6: 779–801.

Gumede, Vusi. 2017. "Leadership for Africa's Development: Revisiting Indigenous African Leadership and Setting the Agenda for Political Leadership." *Journal of Black Studies* 48, no. 1: 74–90.

Hofstede, Geert. 1980. *Culture's Consequences: International Differences in Work-related Values*. Beverly Hills, CA: Sage.

———. 1993. "Cultural Constraints in Management Theories." *Academy of Management Executive* 7, no. 1: 81–94.

House, Robert J. and Ram N. Aditya. 1997. "The Social Scientific Study of Leadership: Quo Vadis?" *Journal of Management* 23: 409–73.

House, Robert J., Paul J. Hanges, Mansour Javidan, Peter W. Dorfman, and Vipin Gupta, eds. 2004. *Leadership, Culture, and Organizations: The Globe Study of 62 Societies*. Thousand Oaks, CA: Sage.

Johnson Sirleaf, Ellen. 2009. *This Child Will Be Great: Memoir of a Remarkable Lady by Africa's First Woman President*. New York: HarperCollins.

Louw, Dirk J. 2002. *Ubuntu and the Challenges of Multiculturalism in Post-apartheid South Africa*. Utrecht: Expertisecentrum Zuidelijk Afrika. www.phys.uu.nl/~unitwin/ubuntu_page.html.

Madimbo, Maggie. 2016. *Transformative and Engaging Leadership Lessons from Indigenous African Women*. New York: Palgrave Macmillan.

Mainah, Fredah and Vernita Perkins. 2014. "Narcissism in Organizational Leadership." Regent University Virtual Leadership Conference.

Mazrui, Ali Al Amin. 1980. *The African Condition: A Political Diagnosis*. London: Heinemann.

Mbigi, Lovemore. 1997. *Ubuntu: The African Dream in Management*. Pretoria: Knowledge Resources.

———. 2005. *The Spirit of African Leadership*. Johannesburg: Knowledge Resources.

Migration Policy Institute. 2012. *Top 10 Migration Policy Issues of 2012*. Migration Information Data Hub. www.migrationpolicy.org/programs/migration-information-source/top-10-migration-issues-2021.

Muchiri, Michael. 2011. "Leadership in Context: A Review and Research Agenda for Sub-Saharan Africa." *Journal of Occupational and Organizational Psychology* 84, no. 3: 440–52.

Ncube, Lisa B. 2010. "Ubuntu: A transformative Leadership Philosophy." *Journal of Leadership Studies* 4, no. 3: 77–82. https://doi.org/10.1002/jls.20182.

Ngugi wa Thiong'o. 1986. *Decolonizing the Mind: The Politics of Language in African Literature.* London: James Currey.

Nkomo, Stella M. 2011. "A Postcolonial and Anti-colonial Reading of 'African' Leadership and Management in Organization Studies: Tensions, Contradictions and Possibilities." *Organization* 18, no. 3: 365–86.

OAU (Organization of African Unity). 1963. *OAU Charter, Addis Ababa, 25 May 1963.* African Union website. https://au.int/en/treaties/oau-charter-addis-ababa-25-may-1963.

Obiakor, Festus E. 2005. "Building Patriotic African Leadership through African-centered Education." *Journal of Black Studies* 34, no. 3: 402–20.

OECD (Organisation for Economic Co-operation and Development). 2020. *International Migration Outlook 2020.* Paris: OECD Publishing. https://doi.org/10.1787/ec98f531-en.

Onukwuba, Henry O. 2018. *Alumni Leadership and University Excellence in Africa: The Case of Lagos Business School.* New York: Palgrave Pivot.

Park, Jong-Dae. 2019. *Re-Inventing Africa's Development: Linking Africa to the Korean Development Model.* New York: Palgrave Macmillan https://link.springer.com/book/10.1007/978-3-030-03946-2.

Senaji, Thomas Anyanje, Elham Metwally, Samuel Sejjaaka, Bill Buenar Puplampu, James Michaud and Hassan Adedoyin-Rasaq. 2014. "LEAD—Leadership Effectiveness, Motivation, and Culture in Africa: Lessons from Egypt, Ghana, Kenya, Nigeria, and Uganda." *Canadian Journal of Administrative Sciences* 31, no. 4: 228–44.

Top 20 Thomas Sankara Quotes, 2018. https://www.youtube.com/watch?v=U6mhQwerRDA.

Zuhmboshi, Nsuh Eric. 2014. "The Rhetoric and Caricature of Social Justice in Post-1960 Africa." *African Literature Today* 32: 91–103.

Chapter 9

LEADER AND LEADERSHIP DEVELOPMENT

We do not have any rights over our planet, simply the obligation to respect, preserve and protect it.

—A Native American philosophy of life

Chapter 9 is an opportunity for the authors to reflect on the major themes from the research, especially that of leadership, and their personal leadership experiences. This chapter further makes a few suggestions on how to improve leadership by focusing on leader development in African countries. The chapter brings to the fore leadership challenges that the researchers have encountered as well as their futuristic approach to handling those issues.

A call for a reengagement with indigenous leadership knowledge, values, and practices is becoming increasingly loud in most of the literature on leader development, especially for African leaders (Bennet et al. 2003; Bolden and Kirk 2009). From their concern for sub-Saharan African leadership, Bolden and Kirk (2009, 71–72) posit that existing leadership and leader development studies, although suggesting that there is an inclination for "cultural preferences within these regions, [...] offer little insight into how people come to conceive of, and take up, a leadership role, or the impacts of this on society." Moreover, those studies are not calling for an African renaissance but rather a rediscovery and a hybrid style of leadership that is Afrocentric and that integrates "African 'indigenous knowledge' with its emphasis on solidarity and interdependence" (Bolden and Kirk 2009, 74).

When asked if he had received any special training for leadership, Martin Luther King replied, "No, I really didn't, I had no idea that I would be catapulted into a position of leadership in the civil rights struggle in the United States. I went through the discipline of early elementary school education and then high school, and college and theological training but never did I realize that I would be in a situation where I would be a leader in what is now known as the civil rights struggle of the United States." (BBC 1961)

Most researchers raise deep and critical questions regarding strategies to be employed in the process of rediscovering, recapturing, reengaging with, and conveying on a global platform this concept of authentic Afrocentric leadership knowledge and practices. To this end, the authors add the questions of brain drain, given the high rate of educated sub-Saharan Africans who emigrate and those of the younger generation who study abroad. Some of those who study abroad, as previously detailed in this book, especially in the chapter of the myth of going back home, never leave, while others are unable to contribute or give back to their families and communities. They also add the consideration of what an authentic African leadership style and leader development program might look like today after all these centuries of influence from former colonizers and imperialists, and the global trend toward a global village. Is there any sense of shared identity and shared aspirations for Africa as there was in the 1960s, given current competing influences? What would a fresh working leadership model for Africa look like? Is Frantz Fanon's wisdom from the 1960s relevant today?

> The future of every man (sic) today has a relation of close dependency on the rest of the universe. That is why the colonized peoples must redouble their vigilance and their vigor. A new humanism can be achieved only at this price. (Fanon 1967, 126)

Outside the UN building stands a huge sculpture declaring the ushering in of a new world order titled accordingly *Breaking Forth from the Old*. With the current global leadership styles that are more rulership and dictatorship than leadership, what does a new world order even mean? Are issues of food security, global climate change, clean drinking water and sanitation, health and well-being (especially given the continued challenges posed by COVID-19, reemerging diseases, and immune microorganisms), peace, human rights, a balance between population growth and distribution of resources, among other dimensions of a good life, all relative?

What value are the rights to freedom and democracy that are often promised by global leaders if defining them is intermingled with terminology that does not clarify how they will contribute to the well-being of all citizens in a global context? What solutions do world leaders have for issues of the unequal status of women, economic inequality, ethnic and religious conflicts, biased media coverage, and an education system that does little to equip us with curiosity and inquiry skills for developing the wisdom to address global issues (not border protectionism)? How is it that global citizens seem to have no voice even when they raise their dissatisfaction through protests? With such a glaring lack of a global vision, a global leadership competency framework, and a capacity to achieve transformative reforms, how can global leaders safely and efficiently meet the growing energy demands and global interaction, and introduce economies that are globally sensitive and yet fair?

Where can we find a mature democracy to model our own after? Research is full of literature of immature and weak democracies whose heads of state are either just posing as democratic leadership or are riddled with oligarchies, militarily dominated, or simply staunchly authoritarian states. Globally, economic, cyber, and environmental crimes have not decreased even with an increase in so-called democratic leadership and sustainability initiatives. Threats from transnational organized crime networks, terrorism and the use of weapons of mass destruction, as well as global initiatives that are not sensitive to human needs, are all too real.

African leaders have consistently failed to learn from the errors of European and American counterparts and continue imitating them blindly, succumbing to the same pitfalls and eventually sabotaging their countries, plunging them into economic and governance confusion or downright chaos and genocide. African leaders, having succeeded in achieving their first goals—whether this be independence, as was the case with the African pioneer leaders, or some of the Millennium Development Goals, including education, health, food security, or other such goals—must now redefine their future goals in line with the needs and sociopolitical dynamics of their countries. It is not enough to revise a constitution if that is not based on an authentic need for self-reflection about the overall welfare of all citizens in the state.

Young people being trained for leadership in Africa should be aware of these dangers and challenges. They should be encouraged to develop character and positive attitudes that will keep them from the pitfalls dug by the previous generation of leaders that prevent the full development of their countries and peoples. Some of the ongoing challenges include dependency on, and blind trust in former colonial and imperial masters, internal and external corruption, nepotism from multinationals and NGOs, underdeveloped infrastructure (and sponsored overpriced construction projects by China and other development partners), and farming and production sectors (some dominated by corrupt multinationals that are supported by their host countries).

Leadership and governance are some of the impediments to Africa's quest for sustainable and equitable development. Explaining such development challenges has continued to elude scholars. To the radical leftist scholars, Africa's underdevelopment can adequately be explained by its forceful and uneven integration into the global economic system. However, with over 50 years of independence, the debate is increasingly focusing on Africa's leadership as a good explanation for its poverty and underdevelopment. The continent should have come of age by now and claimed its identity and place on the planet.

Current poverty levels and underdevelopment in Africa cannot always be viewed from its colonial past and modern imperialism. A culture of enabling has emerged, created by African citizens and leaders themselves by their complacency, support, and imitation of other developed nations instead of seeking homegrown and authentic strategies specific to their issues and that fit Africa's unique characteristics. The search for homegrown strategies was the main theme in the 1970s. What happened to those pioneers of such authentic conversations?

To facilitate their growth and development, future leaders also need to adjust their goals and outcomes. What is leader development, and how does it differ from leadership development? The Center for Creative Leadership (Eckert and Rweyongoza 2015, 1) defines leadership development as capacity expansion aimed at effectiveness in leadership roles or processes, and for increasing one's ability to work with others in productive and meaningful ways. The leadership developmental process is viewed as having three key drivers of leadership development: assessment, challenge, and support (Eckert and Rweyongoza 2015, 12). Leader development program designers and trainers need to design leadership development along these same lines of leader development to reduce the common mistrust and fragmentation that compromises effectiveness, efficiency, and quality in the workplace. Leadership is about the leading person helping the people the leader is working with become focused together on the outcomes of a task. It is not necessarily hierarchical and pyramidal, where one leader has followers, but communal and relational through a collaborative meaning-making process that is continuous and lifelong. These competencies need to become central to leadership in the next decade and beyond.

The definition of African leadership is problematic, as discussed in the previous chapter on leadership. Describing and designing leader development programs is even more problematic. Most researchers of African leadership propose the incorporation of indigenous "African" leadership and management, and its Ubuntu philosophy, into the leader development programs. They argue that if Afrocentric pedagogy and leadership programs are to succeed, they must first be reclaimed and reinstitutionalized in Africa because Eurocentric practices are inadequate and lack the humaneness to meet the challenges in Africa that are embedded in a very different value, cultural, political, economic, and social context. African leadership philosophy is based on sustainable communal practices that are motivated by a spirit of caring for family and community, creating, supporting harmony and hospitality, and respect for all.

As mentioned earlier, Senaji et al. (2014) found in a study of leadership effectiveness that preferred leadership styles involve a hybrid of participative and humane approaches, cultural interaction, solidarity and interdependence, humorous leaders with vision, who are inspiring and at the same time committed to national goals, who are guided by a high level of honesty and transparency, and sensitive to normative differences. How then do we describe, design, and implement leader development systems and programs to equip leaders with such characteristics and while nurturing leaders capable of dealing with the institutional and organizational ills that are unique to the continent? (Senaji et al. 2014).

A Brief Leadership and Management History

Industrial-age definitions of leadership and management are Eurocentric. They focus on individual traits and equate leadership with excellence and one winner, one leader who is powerful because of the position they hold and the influence that gives them power to order everyone else around. Yet, when mistakes occur, the people are blamed and punished, not the leader.

The twentieth century saw the proliferation of more Eurocentric management, work, and organizational studies that mainly focused on the business side and how to maximize profits at the expense of the people. The first organization theories did not emerge until 1920s when Henri Fayol studied organizations from administrative and functional approaches. The organizations themselves focused on labor specialization and mass production and cared less about the effect that they had on employees or the environment.

The end of the century saw some studies like the General Electric/Hawthorne experiments that started to factor in employees. The year 1920 saw the emergence of Elton Mayo's motivation theories, with Peter Drucker's applied management and leadership theory following in 1946 and human relations in the 1950s. Many other management theories emerged from 1946 onward, including Kurt Lewin's organizational development, group dynamics and planned change, Henry Mintzberg's motivation theories, Abraham Maslow's hierarchy of needs in 1954, Frederick Herzberg's two-factor theory in 1959, and Douglas McGregor's X and Y theory of motivation in 1960. However, these theories were viewed as controversial and as supporting laziness. So far, no study has focused on employees' well-being.

In the late 1970s and the 1980s, Tom Gilbert introduced the theory of human performance and technology, Tom Peters helped organizations search for excellence, and Michael Porter studied the value chain although still focusing on business and missing the important point of the consequence of the delight that a product or service by an organization should create for customers or the insightful feedback they could get if they made the customer a key stakeholder. The late 1990s saw the entry of studies on the learning organization by Peter Senge and the boundaryless and virtual organization and expanded globalization policies.

Scientific management by Frederick Taylor set the stage for a systematic approach to organization change. In 1932, the General Electric/Hawthorne studies by Elton Mayo, with his applied behavioral science approach, introduced the importance of the human dimension of organization change and succession. Industrial psychology, and its introduction and integration of the individual and the organization and the proliferation of processes and systems such as survey feedback as a tool kit, sensitivity training, which became prevalent in the 1960s and introduced learning about the self in groups, interpersonal behavior, and group dynamics. Sociotechnical systems, systems theory, and the interdependence of people and organizational work tools were not integrated or studied seriously until 1949 and thereafter.

Organization development and the systematic approach to organization change and leadership came much later. It presented a holistic approach with clear steps and phases and was concerned with humanistic values to guide the entire change and leadership process. Blake and Mouton's managerial grid emerged in 1964, and it became one of the most popular tools for leader development and team training for social interventions such as coercion and confrontation. Indeed, today leader and leadership development is a billion-dollar industry called management consulting (Burke 2007). It also has become the foundation for designing frameworks and indicators for performance and production measurement matrices such as the balanced scorecard and the performance prism that are so common today. These tools and others used today still do not tell us how an employee once appointed to a management position can automatically shift into being an expert on people issues and decide what can and should be measured for employee performance and productivity.

Presenting his punctuated equilibrium paradigm, Gersick (1991) traces the development of change management using aspects of structure, design, strategic orientation, how organization groups and teams develop and work, and the theories that have now become the foundation of change management studies and practice. The author also raised concerns about the inertia that maintains a system's equilibrium and consequently slowing or impeding change efforts.

The twenty-first century is marked by a formalization of the discipline. Tanner and Sternin (2005, 4) recommend a deep and honest analysis of what they call ignored change agents in the employee ranks, using the positive deviance approach where their ideas are harnessed and mainstreamed; leaders lose their big titles and roles of chief discoverer and become learners; bridging the gap between "what is happening and what is possible"; bringing isolated success strategies into the mainstream change management strategies; abandoning the familiar strategies including benchmarking and adopting best practices; countering conventional wisdom that is top-down and shifting blame and responsibility from the corporation and the boss to the individual or community. Brown (2012, 1) concludes "how a leader knows is at least as important if not more important than what a leader knows."

Future change management practitioners need to pay attention to people issues and values such as empowerment and engagement, self-leadership, as well as the slow speed at which leaders embrace learning and acquiring new competencies. Future change management practitioners may also face other twenty-first century leadership challenges such as volatile market forces, globalization, learning techniques, and tools that do not support critical thinking and real-world problem identification and problem-solving techniques.

The Complex Developmental Process of Becoming an Expert Leader

The acquisition of expert levels of knowledge, interpersonal skills, and technical job skills seem to be the foundation for leader development as indicated by the literature and practice. Most organizations have job descriptions that are tiered to three to five levels of proficiency. Proficiency levels for leadership competencies may also be layered in most cases into three to four layers, including information regarding expected duration to achieve, education, certification, training, and skills. Because of this long-held tradition, becoming an expert leader is a complex developmental process that extends over the course of adult development (Day et al. 2012). Skill acquisition does differ when you account for individual differences, self-awareness, self-efficacy, and self-regulatory strength, which may accelerate the learning and development of some leaders. Quinn et al. (2000) assert that changing the self can alter the external world, making self-leadership before organization leadership critical.

Day et al. (2012) offer several hypotheses about leader and leadership development for managing the changes in the world of work. Leadership effectiveness is viewed as the working relationship between the leader and other group members since a single leader cannot inherently possess every quality or leadership dimension necessary to meet the difficult challenges confronting today's rather complex organization leadership. Their four hypotheses state that although nonlinear, the incremental developmental changes in the performance of a leader, to be considered expert, must have occurred over a relatively lengthy time period of up to 10 years or more. They plot the incremental developmental changes as levels where a leader demonstrates continuous growth as they develop through those levels in terms of how quickly they make sense by interpreting and responding as fast as possible to leadership situations while demonstrating complex moral reasoning.

Leader development seems to be linked to adult development on aspects of identity and self-concept, moral development, expert performance, as well as managerial competence. Becoming an expert leader according to Day et al. (2012) is a more than 10 years' complex endeavor. To support their argument, they report that for an individual employee to go through the rigorous preparation for leadership, the process needs to go beyond mastering specific technical competencies of a job. They further argue that unless combined with emotional and social competencies as well as wisdom and strategic competencies, the leader will still not succeed as they should. This is because organizations are complex, and they operate in volatile environments and therefore require more complex ways of thinking and leading. They suggest that leader development interventions start integrating wisdom into leadership curriculum.

To explore the leader proficiency levels further, we compared Day et al.'s work with the Dreyfus Model of Skill Acquisition (1986), which suggests that there are about five stages of skill acquisition. These are based on four qualities: recollection (non-situational or situational), recognition (decomposed or holistic), decision (analytical or intuitive), and awareness (monitoring or absorbed). Just like Dreyfus, Day et al., having considered and factored in individual differences, order the leader proficiency levels into novice, intermediate, and expert.

Based on studies by Day et al. (2012), the following is a general categorization mapped against Dreyfus model:

Basic/entry/novice—A fresh graduate whose competency is in the simplest situations; lacks a sense of the big picture, relies heavily on working memory processes and rules; requires instruction and close extensive guidance. The mode of learning is information processing, non-situational recollection, decomposed recognition, as well as low levels of analytical decision and monitoring of self-awareness. Day et al. confirm this as they offer that expert leadership can be differentiated from novice or emerging leader by the quality of outcomes of a task and by the level of autonomous functioning.

Intermediate/advanced beginner/developing leader—An employee who has been with the organization for at least 2 years and has gained competency to a marginally acceptable level in somewhat difficult situations; requires frequent to occasional guidance and maybe in the leadership mentoring and/or coaching program.

Advanced/competent—An employee who has been with the organization for at least 5 years and has gained leadership experience and knowledge of the kind of response required. May be in a leadership position already and is able to apply the competency in considerably difficult situations; generally, requires little support on decision and choice making and/or no guidance on social skills and behavior. Other skills include fair levels of intuitive decision-making, situational recollection, holistic recognition, analytical decision-making, and increased levels of monitoring self-awareness.

Expert/proficient/mastery—These might be leaders or internal consultants of the organization who possess more sophisticated mental models, are able to apply the competency in exceptionally difficult situations, and serve as a key resource and adviser, coach, and mentor to others. They rely more on environmental-situational and intuitive understanding than on rules and collaboration with others. An individual in this category demonstrates better ability at identifying patterns and analyzing novel situations and processes. To get to this level and maintain it, the expert has a high level of absorbed awareness but still requires continuous training and development that is person-centric. The main factors are how the expert leader practices reflection-on-action and reflection-in-action as well as how they access and use information, manage, and foster positive and constructive work relations.

Day et al. (2012) continue their argument that the development of leadership expertise should be considered and studied as it occurs through the life span, since individuals develop physically, go through identity changes, and grow into adulthood. In their fourth proposition, the authors suggest that leader development should be longitudinal, deliberate, and intentional practice that parallels human development as well job growth as they make their way to the expertise levels. Leader development is therefore viewed as an ongoing process occurring over a life span and shaped by experience and other age-related maturation processes. Others include environmental, political-economic, and social-cultural factors.

One interesting point on career and human development concept that Blustein (2006) raised that links well with the hypothesis of Day and colleagues was that prior to the industrial revolution, choice of work and satisfaction in one's work was a preserve of the rich and landowners, whereas, currently, due to explosion of industrialization and mechanization, and more people being needed to work, the workplace is characterized by high technology, wider knowledge base, digital functioning and automated equipment integrated into globalization and virtual teams, free market capitalism, and fine linguistic lines. The work environments are also changing and starting to focus on quality of work life and well-being, safety, and some benefits.

Leader development needs to be considered as a function of interrelated factors including varieties of developmental experiences that contain some aspects of assessment, challenge, and support; the ability to learn, develop, and grow into expertise, competencies, and eventually skill acquisition; and ability to transfer those to others. Leadership development programs and approaches need to be tailored in such a way that they engage leaders at personal and emotional levels, causing critical self-reflection, and providing support for meaning making, including creating learning and leadership mindsets and experimentation. Developing expertise involves targeted job-specific practice over a period that is focused on overcoming skill weaknesses. Just like any skill development, leadership development requires time and dedication. Indeed, whether it is viewed as a skill, a trait, or a process, one still needs practice to be an expert leader.

In most organizations that follow the traditional hierarchical functional approach of organizing work, employees are hired to fill the needs of the organization along those functions. Work-related cognitive and physical skills as well as personal attributes are scrutinized thoroughly to ensure they are aligned to the teams they will be working with as well as the general organization culture. As employees rise in the hierarchies, they are prepared for leadership roles and responsibilities through training along the levels of proficiency discussed above. Some demonstrate leadership capabilities early on in their career than others. The reason for this is their individual characteristics that make them noticeable to other managers and peers.

Day et al. (2012) proposed that leader development should focus on five primary forms of individual difference variables that influence the leader development spirals, which included self-regulatory strength, learning goal orientation, generalized self-efficacy, self-efficacy, self-awareness, and implementation intentions. Each of the individual characteristics shape and contribute in a special way to leadership development and constitute vocational identity that helps a leader form and keep a clear and stable picture of personal and organizational goals and interests.

The higher one is at the organizational level, the more complex their role becomes and thus the greater the complexity of leader development interventions that are required for the leader to be effective at his/her job (Day et al. 2012). The authors proposed that there is a positive relationship between individual characteristics, abilities, motivation, identity and personality, and leader outcomes that are considered critical by most organizations. Those skills once developed contribute to predicting or enhancing skills acquisition as a function of practice and experience at challenging job assignments as well as leader attributes, including self-efficacy and belief in one's own competency, self-conceptualization and coaching opportunities.

According to Day et al. (2012), effective leadership development strategies should blend job experience, personal characteristics (self-regulation, goal orientation, generalized self-efficacy, self-awareness, and implementation intentions), educational initiatives, job roles, and responsibilities with guided practical experiences such as coaching and mentoring. Day and colleagues add that leadership development should also require performance feedback system and an ongoing process for leader development for everyone in the organization. They suggest that integrating expertise and skill acquisition, social identity, and the self, as well as adult development and learning is a better model of leader development.

Internal and contextual individual factors may exhibit themselves through cognitive and intellectual capabilities as well as experience, personality, affective, value, self-concept and identity, and vocational interests. These may include intra-individual differences and individual changes during development, interpersonal relationships, two-way trust, teamwork, clear objectives, communication, self-belief, courage, integrity, decisiveness, ability to handle change, crisis, and conflicts. Wisdom, a result of exceptional self-development, including ego maturity and post-formal operational thinking (practical and social intelligence), is also part of the individual aspects that influence leader development and efficacy. To support organization goals, some of those individual characteristics can be developed at entry or at first level (bottom level of most triad and hierarchical structures), then effectively implemented at middle and top levels.

Leader skills include problem-solving skills, solution construction skills, and social judgment skills. Those that are the major focus for most leader development programs, according to Day et al. (2012), include technical, which are heavily required at first level, conceptual for top strategic planning and thinking, interpersonal and communication skills needed for every level, and administrative skill, which vary by authority level and type of organization. As demonstrated by the Eurocentric definitions of leadership and management and leader development models discussed above, there is no reference to indigenous African philosophy.

As already said in the previous chapter, African leadership and management is not widely researched and as such there is a lack of indigenous African leader development framework, clear criterion for what constitutes leadership, or a comprehensive competency matrix. This oversight is not due to lack of examples of great democratic leadership in its history, but the heavy dependence and impact of coloniality and modernity.

Lessons learned from these experts on leader and leadership development can be employed to any country if politics and nepotism were set aside. This means that for any aspiring politician, the criteria for offering themselves up for election should not be how much campaign money they raised but how close they are to achieving the criteria discussed above.

From the data collected for this book, our respondents also had some conflicting ideas of their own:

> I came to totally do personal improvement. As a young man, I knew I was multitalented, and my father used to tell me that I would be great. Many things were coming out of me and I realized I could do better by coming to America, with my dreams and as a believer in myself I l realized it was only America that could sustain my faith to improve myself.

> If you come to a new country with a mentality of the other country especially if you take for example Burkina Faso and France and the US. So in order to succeed in that country you have to change your mentality and thinking like the people of the country in order to succeed. When I came here, I think my biggest advantage was I lived only with Americans. Even when I was in France on a scholarship, I had a friend who was from Cameroon with no scholarship and I was shocked because the mentality in Burkina Faso was you go out when you are on a scholarship.

> College education was very competitive in Ethiopia, only top 1 percent got admitted to University. So, when I finished high school, I didn't want to stay there and be a secretary or something like that. I came here with my parents' support.

> I came here because of the opportunity to do my PhD in mathematics education. Mathematics education is not as developed in my country as it is here in terms of research. So, when I got the opportunity for the doctoral program here I took it up for the type of exposure it was going to give me.

> People who have the highest level of resilience make it better here, because when they fall, they wake up. Even though they fall 100 times like Hilary, they come up. It doesn't mean they are perfect but falling is part of a cycle of life because nothing is strived. Here in Michigan, the weather changes 4 times in a year into fall, summer, winter, and everything meaning it doesn't stop life to go on. It is a matter of adjusting to every situation that comes. If it is winter let us put on this. That is how I have realized that they look at life. Their resilience and the entrepreneurship mindset are high. The entrepreneurship mindset helps them or helps all of us to know that you have the full responsibility, not any other person is going to do what you want to achieve, it is you. Even though it is picking grass, collecting stones, driving a tractor but it is your potential. At least, that is what I have learned from them.

What seems evident from the statements above is that various reasons have led to and continue to influence the African brain drain. To solve African leadership problems, Wangari Maathai (2009 introduces a three legged stool framework that includes "democracy, sustainable and accountable management of natural resources, and 'cultures of peace'" (56). According to Maathai (2009), it is the historical, cultural, and economic failure of African leadership to adhere to this framework that mainly contributed to many Africans losing hope and trust in their leaders, and consequently emigrating. To this end she argues that "leadership is an expression of a set of values; its presence, or the lack of it, determines the direction of a society, and affects not only the actions but the motivations and visions of the individuals and communities that make up that society. Leadership is intimately influenced by culture and history, which determine how leadership perceives itself and allows itself to serve: whether it has self-respect, and how it shapes public and foreign policy" (p.25). To her "Leadership is not simply a matter of filling the top positions in a government, institution, or private business" (p.111). Rather, good leadership benefits the people being served and not just the leaders.

Maathai points to the following leadership competencies of honesty, trust, putting people's interest above self-interest, giving people hope, serving for the common good, raising the standards of living and wellbeing for all, problem identification and solving, as key to good governance.

The Value of Power and Influence in Leadership

The use of positive power and influence is the foundation of effective leadership. Effective leaders harness followers' talents and use it for the good of all. In the process they achieve overall organizational desired outcomes and expectations. Behaviors and attributes generally considered, as most effective, most ethical, and most likely to produce such results are generally associated with women. These include emotional intelligence, nurturing, being sensitive, empathetic, intuitive, compromising, caring, cooperative, and accommodative.

An effective leader serves the followers, and by doing so the organization achieves its purpose or bottom line. The leader does so by becoming more aware about social justice issues in the workplace and in the community. Complex and intricate diverse group dynamics are handled through open communication channels and in a free, participative and inclusive manner.

As discussed by Day et al. (2012), one of the individual characteristics that influences leader development is self-regulatory strength. This is the personal ability that an individual uses to direct their cognitive abilities, thinking style, feelings, emotions, attitudes, and behavior in a self-controlled manner that supports personal and organizational goal achievement. Reflective judgment, personal ways of knowing and thinking and understanding of the environment in terms of present and future and other possible scenarios, and taking appropriate action were also emphasized as crucial individual competencies that enhance self-regulatory strength. The reason for that, they argue, is these are the aspects that heavily influence how one views knowledge and truth and shapes their worldview and leadership style.

Blustein (2006) discusses the situational and contextual issues that influence leader development that includes one's background, the culture of the community one grew up in and the dominant culture around them as well as organizational culture. Other characteristics include gender, social and economic status, and education level. Highlighting life contexts and individual backgrounds as part of the individual characteristics, Blustein (2006) suggests applying emancipatory communitarianism in leader development, which emphasizes the explication of personal values and places the focus on an individual's career development and work experiences. Blustein further recommends empowering approaches that promote a sense of community, human diversity and self-determination of individuals.

The next individual characteristic by Day et al. is learning goal orientation, which an individual uses to learn as fast as possible the required capabilities and organization culture and values that they need to be effective leaders. Employees who love to learn new things and are flexible and fast at adapting to change make better leader candidates. Other characteristics include generalized self-efficacy, implementation intentions, and personal self-efficacy, which contribute to one being organized in the way one gathers information, processes it, thinks, makes decisions, conducts oneself, works with others, and organizes work and one's thoughts among others. All these are brought together effectively if one has a high sense of self-awareness and is comfortable in one's identity and who they are. This enables a leader to be authentic in his/her style and lead from the heart as well as from the mind.

Both Maathai (2009) and Day et al. (2012) state that a leader, although an individual, is always working with others and their success is never independent of others input. As such a leader needs to appreciate those who work under them and with them to achieve organization goals, as they are the ones that help the leader to excel. This is an opportunity to exhibit individual characteristics such as self-awareness, self-efficacy, and implementation intentions. This compares well with Mathai's leadership competencies discussed earlier.

Leader Development from Situational and Personal Work Experiences

Both Maathai (2009) and Day et al. (2012) report that leadership efficacy is the belief in one's ability to lead change, set direction, gain commitment, and overcome obstacles to change. Further, they argue that those with higher leadership efficacy seem to seek out more leadership episodes where they can practice and develop leadership.

Arguing that leaders develop in different ways and at different rates, Day et al. (2012) proposed five primary forms of situational and individual difference variables that influence the leader development spirals, which included *self-regulatory strength, learning goal orientation, generalized self-efficacy, self-awareness, and implementation intentions.* They concluded that regardless of the differences, the result of leader development should be an expert level of leadership competence. Others included gender, social and economic status, and education level. The role of choice, access to resources, and ability to make choices were also considered crucial in one's career development path, as well as in leader development.

Leader development, be it formal instruction, self-directed learning, learning-on-the-job, coaching, observing other leaders, or getting feedback from peers and supervisors as well as followers can be learned from job roles that require taking personal responsibility and being accountable. According to Day et al. (2012), individual-based knowledge, skills, and abilities associated with formal leadership roles are the major focus in most leader development programs. These may include interventions that are hoped to influence learning and change through practice and experience. Leader performance in roles and processes is assessed from a leader's behavioral change, self-confidence, accurate self-concept, and self-motivation as well as ability for problem-solving, making quality decisions, quality of interpersonal interactions, language capabilities, social awareness, social skills, ability to learn, and communication among other factors. Collective capabilities such as providing direction, demonstrating alignment, motivating, engaging employees, and generating commitment could also contribute to one's ability to function as a leader. Maathai underscores this idea of collective capabilities when she states that a good leader is one that can step forward, to point out the problems, take responsibility for collective change, offer solutions, and take lead to implement the solutions.

Day et al. (2012) proposed that leadership development includes not only the development of human capital but also the development of social capital. In contrast to human capital, in which the focus is on developing individual knowledge, skills and abilities, social capital builds on networks, and relationships among individuals that enhance cooperation and resource exchange in the organization.

Our respondents were on the mark on this one:

I think success of those who come from Africa because you know we have the same stories, same struggles but people who have been able to attain, and the attainment can be education if that is what they want, starting up business, being economically stable.

[...] getting a piece of people that shows what you know is good, but you have to stay relevant, learn from people who have succeeded, in this age you can learn anything, any subject you know. Someone can write a book with their life story, and you learn it. If you get a degree and you still expect people to do things for you, getting a degree just opens the door and I think that the one thing I can say is for me people like us, no scholarship. Africans who come here already have the will and the determination to succeed. So, the majority of those are successful, but some of them are not. In general the Africans I know in varying levels of success have been able to get a job, support the family and live a better life than what they were living in Africa.

Most people from Nigeria or any African country strive to be not bachelors, masters, PhD or for someone like me I decided to stop at masters because of the nature of my profession. I must get a certification in my job as well. So, their success has always been raising their kids in a good way, being able to send their kids to college, being able to achieve what most people are not expecting most African families to achieve.

As discussed in Chapter 5, issues of decoloniality and fight for epistemic justice need to be resolved organically by Africans themselves without further interference by global superpowers.

Factors Affecting Leader Development

There are many external factors that shape adult and leadership development including national culture, workplace mission and culture, biology and the intersections of body and mind, maturation and aging, psychology, the intersection of spirituality and interpersonal factors, and legal and sociocultural environments. Internal factors of leader development may be contextual or personal and may exhibit themselves through cognitive and intellectual capabilities as well as experience, personality, affective, value, self-concept, and identity, as well as vocational interests. These may include intra-individual differences and individual changes during development, interpersonal relationships, two-way trust, teamwork, clear objectives, communication, self-belief, courage, integrity, decisiveness, ability to handle change, crisis, and conflicts (Yukl, 2014). Because of the way gender and race issues have been polarized worldwide, a leader from a minoritized group faces potential barriers to professional development. The intersectionality issues that such leaders face are only unique to them and not to the leaders from a majority or so-called superior races (Crenshaw, 1989).

Such masculine characteristics, such as being a good decision-maker, organized, assertive, and strategic, have been and continue to be associated with good leadership on one hand. On the other hand, women leaders have been described as sensitive, caring, compassionate, culturally competent, responsive, democratic, participative, collaborative, inclusive, and nurturing. The leadership competencies associated with women are traditionally perceived as incompatible with managerial decision-making roles, which seem to be conceptualized as a function of (a) their socialized traits, behaviors, and styles, and (b) their distinct social location within dominant culture organizations.

Researchers' Reflection on Leadership: Fredah Mainah, PhD

I did not have education or career role models in my life. So I created goals and outcomes that I wanted to achieve in life by using intuition that provided me with divine dissatisfaction. As I grew up and studied, I came across problems and issues that were challenging and I did not have answers or possibilities to work with. On such occasions, I asked myself "What if I am the one responsible for solving this kind of problem, what would I do or think?". As I grew physically, in age and in my career, I was given responsibilities without as much as an hour of training or briefing. I had to quickly learn on the job and learn to ask other colleagues who were in leadership positions how to do certain things. Libraries those days did not have much in terms of management or education and learning theories. Without much process recording to make manuals, and without technology, it was challenging to train those who took over from me. Some of these experiences influenced me to seek further education in areas of human resources management and how to run a business/organization.

In the process I kept reflecting, (without knowing it was even a technique or a widely researched phenomenon and theory), on what I was doing and how I could improve. My career development so far has led me to places I would otherwise never have planned to visit or work at, including several African countries and the United States where I now reside. My career experience spans from teaching high school, to becoming a business development manager, to an even broader consultant for four governments in Africa, to a university professor and internal consultant in the United States. This so far is a tremendous and very satisfying journey and evidence that it is possible to shape one's career path and experiences.

To challenge my growth, I continuously ask myself questions such as:

• What type of leader would I like to be three years from now?
• Does my leadership style reflect who I truly am?

- How can I increase my moments of stretch and yet reduce unnecessary risk and moments of panic?
- How can I translate my episodes of mere competence to excellence?
- What qualities and behaviors do I need to develop without copying anyone?
- How can I inspire others around me to higher levels of excellence in a collaborative manner, without compromising my authenticity and identity and my personal voice?

I build on my strengths and celebrate the values that helped me get there and the victories thus far achieved. I also search for opportunities to keep practicing them. Within the last two years, I have attended conferences and coaching webinars to keep improving. I have also presented at conferences to not only practice but also to network and gain recognition in my field. Further, I keep researching and writing on leadership topics.

For my weak areas, I read more about what research says about those areas and then seek opportunities for improving. Sometimes I feel like I do not have the structural power and social capital to succeed in a country where I am considered as an alien and where the learning curve is so steep and full of challenges. For that I tune into my inner self for confidence. I also try to effectively use my personal power, including expert and referent power within a culture of trust, collaboration and consensus decision-making. Competency, responsibility, and accountability require not only that I make responsible choices and decisions, but also that I demonstrate strength of action by doing what I commit to do.

References

Albert, Michael. 1998. "Shaping a Learning Organization through the Linkage of Action Research Interventions." *Organization Development Journal* 16, no. 3: 29–39.

Bennet, N., Wise, C., Woods, P. A. and Harvey, J. A., 2003. Distributed Leadership: A review of literature. *The Open University, National College for School Leadership: Manchester, UK*. https://oro.open.ac.uk/8534/1/bennett-distributed-leadership-full.pdf.

Block, Peter. 2011. *Flawless Consulting: A Guide to Getting Your Expertise Used*. 3rd ed. Hoboken, NJ: Pfeiffer.

Blustein, David L. 2006. *The Psychology of Working: A New Perspective for Career Development, Counseling and Policy*. New York: Routledge.

Bolden, Richard and Philip Kirk. 2009. "African Leadership: Surfacing New Understandings through Leadership Development." *International Journal of Cross Cultural Management* 9, no. 1: 69–86.

British Broadcasting Corporation (BBC). 1961. "Martin Luther King." An interview by John Freeman. *Face to Face*. BBC Four Talk Collection. www.bbc.co.uk/programmes/p00lgzyl.

Brown, Barrett C. 2012. "Leading Complex Change with Post-conventional Consciousness." *Journal of Organizational Change Management* 25, no.4: 560–75.

Burke, W. Warner. 2007. *Organization Change: Theory and Practice*. Los Angeles, CA: Sage.

Bushe, Gervase R. and Tom Pitman. 1991. "Appreciative Process: A Method for Transformational Change." *OD Practitioner* 23, no. 3: 1–4.

Byrd, Marilyn Y. 2009. "Telling Our Stories of Leadership: If We Don't Tell Them They Won't Be Told." *Advances in Developing Human Resources* 11, no. 5: 582–605.

Combs, Gwendolyn M. 2003. "The Duality of Race and Gender for Managerial African American Women: Implications of Informal Social Networks on Career Advancement." *Human Resource Development Review* 2, no. 4: 385–405.

Cooperrider, David L. and Suresh Srivastva. 1987. "Appreciative Inquiry in Organizational Life." *Research in Organizational Change and Development* 1, no. 1: 129–69.

Crenshaw, Kimberle. 1989. "Demarginalizing the Intersection of Race and Sex: A Black Feminist Critique of Antidiscrimination Doctrine, Feminist Theory and Antiracist Politics." *University of Chicago Legal Forum* Vol. 1989, Article 8. https://chicagounbound.uchicago.edu/uclf/vol1989/iss1/8.

Day, David V., Michelle M. Harrison and Stanley M. Halpin. 2012. *An Integrative Approach to Leader Development: Connecting Adult Development, Identity, and Expertise.* Taylor and Francis. Kindle Edition.

Fanon, Frantz. 1967. *Black Skins, White Masks.* New York: Grove Press.

Eckert, Regina and Simon Rweyongoza. 2015. *Leadership Development in Africa: A Focus on Strengths.* Greensboro, NC: Center for Creative Leadership. https://doi.org/10.35613/ccl.2010.1023.

Gersick, Connie J. 1991. "Revolutionary Change Theories: A Multilevel Exploration of the Punctuated Equilibrium Paradigm." *Academy of Management Review* 16, no. 1: 10–36.

King, Patricia M. and Karen S. Kitchener. 1994. *Developing Reflective Judgment.* San Francisco, CA: Jossey-Bass Publishers

Maathai, Wangari. (2009). *The Challenge for Africa.* New York: Anchor Books.

Moses, Yolanda T. 1989. *Black Women in Academe: Issues and Strategies.* Washington, DC: Association of American Colleges and Universities.

O'Brien, Rory. 2001. "Um exame da abordagem metodológica da pesquisa ação" [An Overview of the Methodological Approach of Action Research]. In *Teoria e Prática da Pesquisa Ação [Theory and Practice of Action Research]*, edited by Roberto Richardson. João Pessoa. Brazil: Universidade Federal da Paraíba. (English version). http://www.web.ca/~robrien/papers/arfinal.html.

Quinn, Robert E., Gretchen M. Spreitzer, and Matthew V. Brown. 2000. "Changing Others through Changing Ourselves: The Transformation of Human Systems." *Journal of Management Inquiry* 9, no. 2: 147–64.

Senaji, Thomas Anyanje, Elham Metwally, Samuel Sejjaaka, Bill Buenar Puplampu, James Michaud and Hassan Adedoyin-Rasaq. 2014. "LEAD—Leadership Effectiveness, Motivation, and Culture in Africa: Lessons from Egypt, Ghana, Kenya, Nigeria, and Uganda." *Canadian Journal of Administrative Sciences* 31, no. 4: 228–44.

Senge, Peter M. 1990. *The Fifth Discipline: The Art and Practice of the Learning Organization.* New York: Doubleday.

Tanner, Richard T. and Jerry Sternin. 2005. "Your Company's Secret Change Agents." *Harvard Business Review* (May 2005): 1–12.

Yukl, G. 2014. *Leadership in Organizations.* Dorling Kindersley, India: Pearson.

Conclusion

APPLICABILITY AND PRACTICAL SUGGESTIONS ABOUT OUR RESEARCH

In this book, we have tried to bring an understanding of the distinctive experiences of sub-Saharan African immigrants as well the diverse and multifaceted challenges that they encounter once they emigrate to the United States. The respondents in this study have shared their stories of relocating, adapting, and coping with their new realities. Storytelling and reflection are not only powerful but also empowering. Giving sub-Saharan African immigrants the opportunity to tell their own stories in their own voices empowers them in an authentic way to become agents of their own lives. This results in the ability to forge a meaningful future for themselves. Moreover, their lived experiences will provide helpful lessons to future immigrants as they navigate their immigration journey.

We argued that acknowledging the historical nature of racial bias and White privilege in the United States without taking time to examine issues of race and privilege or considering the importance of cultural diversity is detrimental to all. Coming from countries where Blackness is not a point of reference, the sub-Saharan African immigrants are somewhat oblivious to racism and discrimination at first. Later, they come to realize that racism is a constant reality they have to deal with on a daily basis. Dealing with race thus becomes an important component of how they adjust to their new lives as immigrants. Even those who adapt fast eventually realize they will never be American enough going by the racially charged definitions and expectations.

Personal effort, determination, and eventual success of sub-Saharan African immigrants continue to be underappreciated independent of historical colonization, marginalization, stereotypes, and tokenism among other stigmas. These stigmas cause sub-Saharan African immigrants to be viewed as not being proactive or possessing agency in the process of personal purpose and self-determination. Sub-Saharan African immigrants are therefore constantly faced with situations that require them to debunk these myths or conform and exhibit the stereotypical images society has imposed on them.

Based on the challenges experienced by our respondents as discussed in this book, we as engaged scholars realized that there is a need for supporting and coaching sub-Saharan African immigrants to succeed and to continuously create conditions and institutional interventions that foster their integration, assimilation, and success in their host countries. Currently, they have little to no access to role models or mentors who they can rely on to help them adjust to life in their host countries, successfully navigate higher education and graduate, get meaningful work, and have a higher quality of life. Most coaching models and materials available are modeled on Eurocentric learning and thinking styles.

Using a non-Eurocentric coaching model such as the Sankofa Model would be more effective for sub-Saharan African immigrants. Sankofa is an Akan word, which means to reflect on one's past in order to inform one's future. Our adopted Sankofa Model requires recalling and reflecting on one's past, understanding it, and designing future development strategies from the insights gained from the reflexive exercise.

Most coaching programming using the Sankofa Model that is available is designed for African American males (Jarjoura 2013; Gibson 2014). There are not many materials available that coach using non-Eurocentric models like the selected Sankofa method. This Africa-centered Sankofa Coaching Model is not a common one and as such there are no readily available coaching materials designed toward minoritized groups. Therefore, there is a need to develop a more inclusive Sankofa Model tailored to the specific needs of all minoritized groups. The model is based on three dimensions: (1) self-actualization through personal reflection and determination; (2) personal awareness and sociological imagination about the intersectional nature of race, class, and gender issues; and (3) the need for communal support from a Black cultural perspective viewed as sisterhood, other-mothering, and mothering of the mind. This requires for the mentor-coach to be one who prepares the future generations of sub-Saharan African immigrants for continuity and sustainability.

In an attempt to give the participants a voice about their experiences and affirm the role their own efforts and agency plays in their success, our Sankofa Model is also influenced by interpretivism. The Sankofa Coaching Model will be used as an intervention and approach to coaching to help sub-Saharan African immigrants succeed in their host countries. Cultural perspectives that are unique to sub-Saharan African immigrants will be used to design interventions for them. We posit that coaching using our Sankofa Model that is close to sub-Saharan African immigrants' values will intervene and increase the rate of success. Programming using the Sankofa Model is unique and adaptable for any group, but more effective for minoritized groups whose backgrounds and cultures are more community oriented. Without communal support systems, sub-Saharan African immigrants may face challenges when navigating a huge community that is different from their own.

Limitations and Future Research

Future research should explore the role gender plays not only in understanding the specific challenges sub-Saharan African men and women experience but also the different coping strategies they each develop. Gender roles, expectations, and cultural values might lead women to have a harder time adjusting and coping in their host countries compared to their male counterparts. Additionally, future research should explore health and wellness of sub-Saharan African immigrants, the elusive American dream, the distinctive experiences of sub-Saharan African immigrants, and other dimensions of transnational identity.

Some of those denials, especially among sub-Saharan women immigrants, that seem to stem from their unique cultural value and belief systems, as well as the clash of those values with values prevalent in the United States, remain relatively under-researched. Consequently, breaking the silence and denials around those cultural practices will tremendously help future immigrants cope better and know what to expect once presented with similar circumstances.

Recommendations

Our respondents who were students made a few recommendations, which they felt would improve college life for them and other future international students. Those recommendations include a social program with a centralized place equipped for African immigrants to help them adjust and integrate into the higher education environment in the United States, to navigate campus, determine success, get a campus job, maintain immigration status, achieve academic success, get food cheaply, apply for international scholarships and find events on campus, career opportunities, and information on companies that employ students legally. The center was most important to them because it would help them solve all the other challenges of being homesick, missing deadlines on school assignments because they did not know how to navigate the electronic resources and dropping out due to economic hardships.

The researchers concurred with the participants especially about a student success center with a program that supports immigrant students' success by focusing on their unique needs. For most international students from developing countries, once their parents or sponsors pay tuition, there are no allowances provided for the student. Expanding job opportunities on and off campus would give them access to necessities that the university does not provide like food and accommodation as well as books.

Respondents who were not students suggested that immigration reforms and policies be more friendly and welcoming to immigrants from sub-Saharan Africa. This would make their integration less challenging. Specifically, they suggested making sure that all immigrants get an initial orientation to American culture, values, language skills, and job and skills training. Other suggestions included peer counseling and mentoring of newly arrived African immigrants by fellow Africans who are already settled.

It was evident throughout our research that being a sub-Saharan African immigrant poses unique challenges. Apart from isolation, loneliness, and missing family and community support, adjusting to the weather and different cultures were among the major challenges cited. Economic challenges were also a major hindrance to student success.

A phenomenologist approach to research is also challenging. Being involved and immersing oneself too intensely in the research can introduce unintended bias. Data collection becomes a huge endeavor because of the large amount of data collected. Analyzing and interpreting without introducing personal bias was the greatest challenge. Bracketing was very helpful to the researchers.

From a phenomenological constructivist perspective, mature individuals make meaning of their surroundings by examining and evaluating relevant information, opinion, experience and available explanations (the process of reflective thinking), then constructing plausible solutions for the problem they need to solve. Individuals create meaning for themselves or make sense of new information by planning, selecting, organizing, and integrating information with other knowledge, often in the context of social interactions. Individual constructivism involves constructing knowledge through personal cognitive processes and their own experiences, not necessarily by memorizing facts.

When an individual is in a group or a community, the knowledge and experience construction changes as it gets influenced by the interaction between the knowledge they bring to a situation and social or cultural exchanges within that content and context (King and Kitchener 1994; Day et al. 2012). Meta-cognitive reflection encourages reevaluation of beliefs and to periodically think about the ways that these beliefs have changed overtime. Most individuals as knowers are constantly involved in social relations and interactions that are generally hierarchical where they might have little power and/or autonomy, steeped in historically and culturally specific contexts and thus resulting in experiences that are a byproduct of power relations (Day et al. 2012).

This book shared the specific lived experiences of sub-Saharan African immigrants, a group which, although it makes up a great majority of African immigration to the United States, remains understudied. The stories we told in this work therefore significantly contribute to the debates about immigrations laws and policies especially those regarding sub-Saharan African immigrants.

References

Jarjoura, G. R. 2013. Effective Strategies for Mentoring African American Boys. American Institutes for Research. Retrieved from http://www.air.org/sites/default/files/downloads/report/Effective%20Strategies%20for%20Mentoring%20African%20American%20Boys.pdf.

Gibson, Y. 2014. The Impact of Mentoring Programs for African American Male Community College Students. *Journal of Mason Graduate Research* 1, no. 2: 70–82.

INDEX

CPSIA information can be obtained
at www.ICGtesting.com
Printed in the USA
LVHW090905240723
753027LV00079B/36